Boxing Like the Champs 2

More Lessons from Boxing's Greatest Fighters

Mark Hatmaker

Jack Johnson

Tracks Publishing
Ventura, California

Cover: Joe Louis and Max Schmeling
Library of Congress

Boxing Like the Champs 2
Lessons from Boxing's Greatest Fighters
Mark Hatmaker

Tracks Publishing
458 Dorothy Avenue
Ventura, CA 93003

tracks@cox.net
www.startupsports.com
trackspublishing.com

Copyright © 2020 by Mark Hatmaker and Doug Werner
10 9 8 7 6 5 4 3 2 1

Publisher's Cataloging-in-Publication

Hatmaker, Mark, author.

Boxing like the champs 2 : more lessons from boxing's greatest fighters / Mark Hatmaker.

Ventura, California : Tracks Publishing, [2020] I An update and continuation of "Boxing like the champs" (Tracks Publishing, c2016). I Includes bibliographical references and index.

ISBN: 978-1-935937-80-7 (trade paper) I 978-1-935937-81-4 (epub) I 978-1-935937-82-1 (mobi) I 978-1-935937-83-8 (PDF) I LCCN: 2020938543

LCSH: Boxing. I Boxing—History. I Boxing—Psychological aspects. I Boxers (Sports)—Training. I Boxers (Sports)—Training—History. I Boxers (Sports)—Psychological aspects. I Boxers (Sports)—Biography. I LCGFT: Biographies. I BISAC: SPORTS & RECREATION / Boxing.

LCC: GV1137.6 .H385 2020 I DDC: 796.83—dc23

Books by Mark Hatmaker

No Holds Barred Fighting:
The Ultimate Guide to Submission Wrestling

More No Holds Barred Fighting:
Killer Submissions

No Holds Barred Fighting:
Savage Strikes

No Holds Barred Fighting:
Takedowns

No Holds Barred Fighting:
The Clinch

No Holds Barred Fighting:
The Ultimate Guide to Conditioning

No Holds Barred Fighting:
The Kicking Bible

No Holds Barred Fighting:
The Book of Essential Submissions

Boxing Mastery

No Second Chance:
A Reality-Based Guide to Self-Defense

MMA Mastery:
Flow Chain Drilling and Integrated O/D Training

MMA Mastery:
Ground and Pound

MMA Mastery:
Strike Combinations

Boxer's Book of Conditioning & Drilling

Boxer's Bible of Counterpunching

Mud, Guts & Glory
Tips & Training for Extreme Obstacle Racing

She's Tough
Extreme Fitness Training for Women

Boxing for MMA

Boxing Like the Champs

*Books are available through major bookstores
and booksellers on the Internet.*

This one is for Doug. A good man who allows me to rattle on endlessly about these combat sports that I love so well.

And to you, Dear Reader. Anyone who takes the time to read this volume, or any of the others by Yours Truly, I am deeply grateful.

This book would not have been possible without Kylie Hatmaker and Scott "Bulldog" Ritch.

Contents

How to use the Boxing Mastery manuals 7
Intro: Condemn yourself 9

How to use the Boxing Mastery manuals

This book and the others in this series are meant to be used in an interlocking, synergistic manner where the sum value of the manuals is greater than the individual parts. What we are striving to do with each manual is to focus on a specific aspect of the sport and give thoughtful consideration to the necessary ideas, tactics and strategies pertinent to the facet of focus.

We are aware that this piecemeal approach may seem lacking if one only consumes one or two manuals at most, but we are confident that once three or more manuals have been studied, the overall picture or method will begin to reveal itself.

Since the manuals are interlocking there is no single manual in the series that is meant to be complete in and of itself. They are all made stronger by an understanding of the material that preceded it. And so on and so forth with each manual in this series. Now, let's lace up those gloves!

A note from the deep south

You will notice in these photos that I box southpaw. I'm a natural righty who retrained southpaw to put coordinated/power-side forward and to beef up my "weak" hand. In other words, I sincerely see power-side forward as not losing a power hand, but putting power into both hands.

Nowhere in these pages will you find me preaching to you to make the switch. I just bring up my obvious southpaw stance for the question that usually follows: "I'm an orthodox fighter, will this book work for me?" Yep. No worries, boxing is boxing. Southpaws, follow my lead, literally. Orthodox fighters, flip the photos in your mind and we're all on the same page.

Condemn yourself

You've likely heard this quote before…

"Those who cannot remember the past are condemned to repeat it."

…for the fighter, to be truly condemned to repeat the historic magic of these great ring men, we will have to take it to the gym...

It was uttered by the Spanish philosopher George Santayana. In context, he issued it as a warning to those who seek solutions on the world stage, urging them to have a bit of longview perspective before they plunge on merrily or madly with this or that "save the world" scheme.

In that context Mr. Santayana was likely sage. But on this smaller stage of a canvas covered ring, bordered by ropes and turnbuckles, it is a bit of untruth. Oh, but only if it were true for we lovers of fistic mayhem.

Ponder that quote again:

"Those who cannot remember the past are condemned to repeat it."

How sweet it would be to know nothing of the artistry, the craftiness, the wisdom of the past masters of the sweet science and through sheer ignorance to simply blunder into their mastery. Sounds nice, but who are we fooling? To know how these warriors did what they did, to really know, you've got to look, you've got to study, you've got to dig, you've got to work hard to know their past. In our case, it is only by knowing the past that we condemn ourselves to repeating it. No knowledge of it, well, then it simply ain't gonna happen by magic.

In this follow up to the first volume, *Boxing Like the Champs*, we will use our definition of "condemn" to grab a piece of history and repeat it to the best of our ability. Contained herein are training tips, ring tactics, "secret" punches, strategies, and more than a few "dirty tricks" peppered here and there. They are offered in no particular order. In other words, dip and dive where your particular fist-waving taste swings you for that given training day.

I do offer this caveat. This book can be read as mere history or strategic maundering, but for the fighter to be truly condemned to repeat the historic magic of these great ring men, we will have to take it to the gym, to the bags, to the pads, to the sparring partners. Words on pages do not translate into ability any more than being ignorant of history condemns us to repeating it.

Read on, work hard and condemn yourself to a bit of historic mastery!

Part 1

Tactics

1. "Susie-Q" x 2

Rocco Francis Marchegiano.
aka Rocky Marciano.
aka The Rock.
aka The Brockton Blockbuster.

A bona fide claimant to the pantheon of all-time greats. What can be said about this champ that you don't already know? He's the only heavyweight champ to retire unde-

feated: 49-0. At 43 KOs he has the highest knockout percentage of any heavyweight champion in history. Some quibble that he couldn't have beat some of the greats of the past or those that came after, but to all those quibblers, he fought the best around at his time and that's the job. He did this while standing five foot eight (some put the height at five-ten, but that's a bit of wishful thinking). He weighed in around 188 pounds. He had a paltry reach of 68 inches. And yet, The Rock could put them away.

We could talk his work ethic, his chin, his embracing of the grind, but let's talk that big right hand of his he dubbed, "Susie-Q." If we take a surface cursory look at the way

Rocky threw Susie-Q we may be tempted to walk away shaking our heads at the inelegance of his technique and chalk its success up to mere strength, brutality and a long stretch of luck. But we keener-eyed fighters see something more than a mere wild, looping, lucky rear hook.

First, what many label a rear hook is not, in fact, a hook at all. It is a two-punch conglomerate. At times it is a straight right hand, at others it is a bit of a looping overhand. So why is Susie-Q so often described as a hook? It comes down to the Rock's diminutive stature and unorthodox movement that cause many to interpret the end result as a hook.

Setting up Susie-Q

The Rock would extend that lead arm and protect his face with the rear hand. He would accompany this protective posture with deep bobs to his inside (to his right or a southpaw's left.)

He used these deep bobs to protect his head and make his opponents miss. What did make it through often glanced off his brow. He also used that crouch to the inside to fire his Susie-Qs from the floor. As he came out of the deep bob, that rear hand would unfurl as either a big rear straight or a chopping overhand.

Both punches traveled closer to a straight line than do a looping rear hook, thus making this "inelegant" boxer a bit more elegant in that by choosing the straight path with both forms of Susie-Q he was still being wisely defensive with this often devastating offense.

11 rounds to Susie-Q x 2
Round 1
● Hit the mirror and assume the Rock's extended lead and face-covering rear hand posture.
● Start working deep bobs to the inside making sure that you take your hands with you and don't leave your head exposed.

Rounds 2-3
● Repeat round one.

Yes. Head and hand move in sync.

No. Head exposed.

Rounds 3-5

● Using the heavy bag or a pad feeder, implement the lessons of the first three rounds to start firing the rear straight version out of the deep crouch.

Rounds 6-8
● Work on making that Susie-Q travel the short choppy overhand path.
● Do not curl it from the outside, but over the top in a straight path.

Rounds 9-11
● Stay on the bags or pads and mix your Susie-Qs.
● Strive to make them flow easily out of your upper body movement.

After those eleven rounds you're just like The Rock. That is assuming, you are as hard working and gritty and powerful as he was.

OK, so maybe we're not The Rock, but closer everyday is a good day.

Library of Congress

2. Joe Louis & "Brewster style"

Joe Louis, aka The Brown Bomber, was, is and always will be one of the indisputable greats in heavyweight history. He held the belt for an incredible twelve years (1937-1949) and this was no duck-and-cover version of holding the title where you win it and then take a fight or two here and there to keep the laurels and cash coming in. Louis put up 26 successful defenses of his belt which is pretty damn active. That active champion's record comes in second only to the superb Julio Cesar Chavez who had 27 title defenses.

Now, what is it that made Joe Louis so great?

Actually, that's the wrong question since it is asked in the singular. It's not what one thing made Louis so great, it's a combination of more than a few attributes. We'll cover a few in this volume, but let's start with something foundational to his approach—"The Brewster style."

Now, we're not exactly sure who coined the term Brewster style, but we do hear it coming from the lips of the legendary trainer Walter Smith who was in Joe Louis' stable. The "Brewster" Smith was referring to was not a person but a place—The Brewster Recreation Center in Detroit, Michigan.

> It's how you put these ingredients together that let us know if we've got a habanero hot chili or a warmed-over stew.

This gym saw many a good fighter walk through its doors. And under that roof there was a bread and butter boxing foundation that was instilled in fighters from day one. The trainers who were the authors of this Brewster Style were Atler Ellis and Holman Williams.

Now what exactly was the Brewster style? Let's have Walter Smith define it for us.

"Left jab, right hand, left hook. Boxing all the time. Moving back and forth. This is the Detroit style. You gotta have a good left hand. That's the Detroit style."

Sounds simplistic doesn't it? But far from it the deeper we get. Boxing is straights and hooks, uppercuts and an overhand here and there. Not a lot of ingredients, but the recipe is still mighty powerful. It's how you put these ingredients together that let us know if we've got a habanero hot chili or a warmed-over stew.

Let's shoot for spicy hot chili Brewster style.

12 rounds of Brewster style
Round 1
Jab/ cross /lead hook in the mirror. Look for snap and not getting overextended. Don't strive for variety, stick to the Brewster style basics. Don't sweat your footwork, yet.

Round 2

Another round of mirrorwork, but this time do it thusly…

- Step jab
- Step jab/ cross
- Step jab/ cross/ lead hook
- Repeat

Step outside jab

Step outside jab and cross

Step outside jab, cross and lead hook

Round 3

More mirrorwork.
- Step outside jab.
- Step outside jab/ cross
- Step outside jab/ cross/ lead hook

Step inside jab

Step inside jab and cross

Step inside jab, cross and lead hook

Round 4

More mirrorwork.

- ● Step inside jab
- ● Step inside jab/ cross
- ● Step inside jab/ cross /lead hook

Step back jab

Step back jab and cross

step back jab, cross and lead hook

Round 5

More mirrorwork.
- Step back jab
- Step back jab/ cross
- Step back jab/ cross/ lead hook

Round 6
More mirrorwork.
● This time, put it all together.
Improvise your footwork, but stick
to the Brewster basics.

Rounds 7-12
● Take it to the pads and work
rounds 1-6 in this same stairstep
manner.

By the time you are done with
this workout you will have thrown
36-minutes of non-stop Brewster
basics. And put your feet working
for you just like the Brown
Bomber and the other pupils of
Atler Ellis and Holman Williams.

Those are some fine historical
footsteps to walk in.

3. Joe Louis' step & throw

Joe Louis was a heavy hitter.

How heavy? In a total of 69 fights we've got 52 knockouts. Those he did not knock out can attest that it wasn't for lack of trying on the champ's part and they did their best to stay away from those heavy, heavy hands. In 2004 *The Ring Magazine* offered a list of the "100 Greatest Punchers of All-Time." Topping that list? Yeah, you guessed it, Joe Louis.

> "...Blackburn taught him that if you step in with that punch how much more effective it would be..."
>
> —Freddie Guinyard

So where did that power come from? Sure, a lot of it was an attribute of Louis himself, he was a big solid powerful athlete. Was it the Brewster style that made his power? Not necessarily, although it didn't hurt. It seems that what took Louis' natural gift for good heavy hands and pushed it even further was the addition of a tactic instilled in the Brown Bomber by his trainer, Jack Blackburn.

Blackburn was no slouch as a fighter himself, but it is his work with Louis that he is particularly known for. Blackburn recognized Louis' natural gifts and added a component from his own fighting days that was a tried and true tactic for gaining punching power and put his gifted pupil through the paces to make it second nature.

What was this powerful tactic? Step with your punches.

Blackburn advised and drilled Louis to whenever and wherever possible step in with each and every punch. These steps were not the exaggerated falling steps that we find in Jack Dempsey's style, but more of a deliberate, balanced movement accompanying every punch.

Freddie Guinyard, Joe Louis' boyhood friend, travel companion and secretary, offered that it was Blackburn who took his friend's natural power and added the step-punch factor.

"Blackburn worked on the whole body movement—to step in while throwing a punch. [as an amateur] Joe would stand back and he was so powerful that he could throw a punch and knock a man out, but Blackburn taught him that if you step in with that punch how much more effective it would be."

With Blackburn's power-punching wisdom in mind, let's overlay his advice with the Brewster style we've already drilled.

Step jab

Step jab and step cross

Step jab, step cross and step lead hook

Ten rounds of Blackburn + Brewster style

Round 1 / Mirrorwork

- Step jab
- Step jab/ step cross

  Step jab/ step cross/ step lead hook

  Repeat
- Admittedly some of these steps may be abbreviated, but find a small step-in all the same.

Round 2

Repeat the preceding construct with outside steps.

Round 3

Repeat with inside steps.

Round 4

Repeat with retreating steps.

Strive to find the right timing where the rear foot plants and uses a slight calf boost to power each punch.

Round 5

- Freeform your Brewster style but strive to put a step into each and every punch.

Rounds 6-10 / Heavy bag

Repeat rounds 1-5 on the heavy bag really looking for that powerful punch-step timing.

- Strive for the punch landing as the foot makes solid canvas contact.

Now, of course, it will be impossible to step with each and every punch in actual sparring and matches, but if we drill the above assiduously we will find that we will be stepping far more often, far more actively and with far more power than we formerly did.

Thanks for the powerful tip, Mr. Blackburn!

4. Joe Louis' balancing act

What, another tip from the Brown Bomber?

Hell yeah! The past masters provide us with so much gold to be mined—a wealth of material to inform our present-day training. So it is wise to keep digging and reaping rewards as often as possible.

> "...but most important, balance if I missed. Balance in action was his god."
>
> —Joe Louis on trainer Jack Blackburn.

We know that Louis was rock solid in his style, Brewster solid to be exact. We know that he had power thanks to Jack Blackburn's schooling on his step-and-punch method.

Louis also had speed. For a big man he put some quick movement together. Speed is often an inborn attribute. It can be helped along by smooth efficient drilling, but for the most part speed is a God-given gift. But there is an attribute of speed that can be hacked and developed. That speedy attribute is balance.

Let's have a listen to trainer Walter Smith and what he saw as Jack Blackburn's biggest assist to Joe Louis:

"He taught him balance…As long as a man keeps himself on balance when throwing punches—that is one of the basic things of boxing. If you don't have good balance, your punches are not going to be effective."

But let's not take Smith's word on Blackburn's insistence on balance. This is the Brown Bomber himself on what he felt was Blackburn's greatest advice:

"You ask me what one great thing he taught me stands out in my mind? It was the trick of balance, balance in setting to hit, balance in delivering a punch, balance after I landed, but most important, balance if I missed. Balance in action was his god."

Are you hearing that? "Balance in action was his god."

Which, in turn, became one of Louis' self-admitted vital tools. So how do we make balance an important part of our own game?

Lightweight bag

A heavy bag is a staple of boxing training. There is nothing like it to develop power. The bigger the bag that you can manhandle, the better.

But to develop balance in delivering heavy hands, it is wise to spend time on bags waaaaay lighter than you would usually consider. For instance, if you commonly work a 90-100-pound bag, spend a like amount of time on say a 40-pound bag. Ideally, you will throw just as hard as you did on the bigger bag and not adjust for the lightness.

Resolving to throw heavy despite the smaller size will give us more sway and create more chaotic angles allowing us to "find our balance" in the midst of misses, near misses and bag grazes. Use the following bag rotation to keep a good balance of speed and power.

The heavy to light bag 6-round rotation
Round 1
Bang the big bag HARD and FAST.

Round 2
Bang the light bag HARD and FAST. Strive to make no let off in speed or power. There will be more misses and awkward moments initially but that's OK. That's part of the balance learning process.

Rounds 3-6
Alternate this for two more cycles.

The make 'em miss focus drill protocol
This is not so much a set drill as an addition for your trainer or pad feeder to make part and parcel of practically every focus mitt session.

The feeder is occasionally, at his whim, to flash the mitt calling for a punch, but as the punch comes in deprive the mitt. The goal is to teach the fighter to always find balance and good recovery when throwing hands—to never feel off balance. Often fighters only miss in the ring where being out of balance matters greatly. Programming your gym training for misses with bag work and mitt work allows you to get a bit closer to reality and start making balance in action one of your own demigods.

5. "Biting," bare-knuckle boxing & Jack Johnson's biceps punch

First things first, this sermon on "biting" has nothing to do with your teeth, so rid yourself of images of Mike Tyson chowing down on Evander Holyfield's ear. In early frontier rough & tumble parlance, biting was to take a shot at your opponent's punching arm with your own fist—specifically an incoming fist. (There is an entirely different rough & tumble vocabulary for injuring your opponent's arms while in the passive, defensive or on guard position which we will discuss in a bit.)

> It takes only one or two bites of your opponent's arms to begin mitigating his or her power game...

You will find a few references to biting as a not necessarily on the square tactic in the early days of bare-knuckle work in Merrie Old England. It made its transfer across the pond with some fighters making it a feature of their work. In American frontier rough & tumble there was no onus or pretension of "That's not quite cricket" since more often than not all-in fighting was just that. Let's face it, in an era and fighting method that prided itself on numerous ways to scoop eyes, taking a shot at your opponent's arms was child's play.

The tactic survived into the early gloved era where it was often hidden as a less than kosher blow, but some made no bones that it was part and parcel of their arsenal. The legendary Jack Johnson made training the "biceps punch" as he called it a standard part of his training camp.

The bite or biceps punch is almost exclusively a lead hand blow and can be thrown in four primary ways.

1. As a short lazy jab to the biceps of the incoming punching arm.
2. As a loose open hook to the biceps.
3. As an elongated backfist or hammerfist.
4. As a rising hammerfist when the lead arm is in a down reference point as in a Philly cover.

Biting has an easy correlate in the "gunt" of Filipino martial arts and the "defanging the snake" concept that runs through practically every combat school no matter the hemisphere of origin. Whereas the gunt often has a rear hand assist or the use of the offensive rear hand as well, the bite as used in early boxing is a lead hand tool, and seldom if ever will you see the rear hand adding to sending the limb off track.

The old school bite will appear almost invisible. That is, it appears to be a loose aspect of a reaching defense. If one will call to mind the great boxer Tommy Loughran's "jab and a half" method of fighting as we detailed in the first book in this series, *Boxing like the Champs*, you will have a very good idea of how to throw such an animal.

Loughran's jab was always accompanied by a reaching defense with the rear hand. Now, Loughran's jab was kosher seeking legal targets, but that rear hand used as an aggressive adjunct of defense is on the correct page.

If we look to Jack Johnson's rocked back "picking off the

punches" style we can see the ideal form of biting. To bite as Johnson did, we would shift slightly out of range, hold the hands high, allow the rear hand to lay back and play catches, pats, cuffs and muffles while the lead hand loosely sought to find the incoming biceps of either arm.

One does not have to put a lot of power into biting. The stink of the bite comes from the opponent's own power. If he swings that hook hard, your loose hooking bite is merely acting as a punch in a head-on biceps collision.

The bite offers many attractive qualities:
- A good offensive-defensive game.
- Allows the shorter fighter to skip worries about reach.
- Allows the taller fighter to emphasize reach.
- Saves hands — smacking on biceps is far easier on the metacarpals than colliding with craniums.
- Slows your opponent's roll. It takes only one or two bites of your opponent's arms to begin mitigating his or her power game since the new factor of limb injury comes into play.
- It's an easy "hide." By that, I mean when played well it's almost impossible to tell you are using a biting strategy from the outside. And when facing a good biter it is almost invisible because biting looks like defense, which it is, but a defense that, well, bites and bites hard.

I highly suggest resurrecting this formidable and easily educated old school tool.

Five rounds to biting and biceps punching prowess

Round 1

Have your feeder lace on some 16 oz. gloves and throw lazy shots at you. Strive to use the rear hand for defense and the lead hand to fire lazy jabs into the incoming punches. (BTW the feeder is throwing lazy for his or her protection. Biting adds up fast, be kind to one another.)

Round 2

Repeat the lazy feeds, but here we will strive to make our bites loose hooks. Again, no need for power, your opponent's power will do the job.

Round 3

Repeat lazy feeding, but here use a lazy backfist into the incoming biceps.

Round 4

With the lead hand in a low guard, use a rising backfist to bite biceps and triceps.

Round 5

Now the drilling becomes reciprocal. You will spar one-for-one. That is, Boxer A looks for a target and fires, while Boxer B defends and looks for a bite. Then Boxer B looks for a target and fires, Boxer A looks for a bite. This tit-for-tat without combinations allows you to emphasize the bite and slow your roll so we don't take on too much damage.

Double-end biting

I have found that focused biting rounds on the double-end bag is an excellent solo practice to build this facility. Simply lay back, Jack Johnson style, punch the bag into motion and begin looking for lazy bites.

Biting with jab.

Biting with hook.

Biting with backfist

Biting with rising backfist.

6. Movement-under-load training

Let's take a journey from the ancient Olympics, stop by Denmark for some Viking practices, sojourn with the Inuit and Chippewa cultures, and steal yet more ideas from the boxing heavyweight great, Joe "The Brown Bomber" Louis.

First, let's define our terms. By movement-under-load training I refer not to weight lifting, but the conducting of your training with additional weight or added resistance hampering your standard movement in the aid of increasing performance once the limiter is removed.

Ancient Hellenes

In the original incarnations of the Olympic Games, the jumping events, standing broad jump, running jump, clearing obstacles, et cetera were conducted with devices called halteres. Halteres were bits of stone or metal loosely shaped like a modern dumbbell. The athlete would grasp the two ends of the haltere and use a swinging momentum of the arms to "assist" the jump without ever releasing the device. It was thought that halteres would increase strength and difficulty.

I've tried it and it does, although experimenting with mock haltere (grasping a dumbbell) my swinging jump coordination left much to be desired, and the landing g-forces made me leery of attempting maximal efforts. However, no less a personage than Aristotle in his *On the Movement of Animals* states, "A pentathlete using halteres jumps farther than one without them." Gradually these devices faded from being used in the games, but were still used in the training of the "jumpist" (an archaic word I have grown fond of).

Fjords of Scandinavia

There are numerous references in the sagas to Vikings training in knee and waist high water. They would run, jump and engage in mock combat in this depth to both garner strength and to train in conditions they were likely to encounter in storming beaches.

There are numerous references in the anthropological record of Northern tribes, the Inuit and Aleut among them, competing in running and sprinting in various depths of snow. Here the snow acts in the same resisting manner as does the melted form in the Viking counterpart of the training. As a matter of fact, roadwork in high snow was an aspect of Joe Louis' training.

American Indian tribes have a deep and resonant history of running. Running for war training, running for escape training and running for ritualized purposes. Many tribes had their own form of adding resistance to the runs ranging from partner carries, stone hauls, creek running (the Viking idea rears its head again), running in deep sand along dunes and hill and mountain running.

But let us look to the Chippewa tribe for a specific device to add resistance. As part of a tradition linked to the deity Part-Sky Woman, runners would attach decorative weights filled with lead shot to the bare feet. Many miles were run with these ankle weights, but they were shed for tribal competition or warfare.

20th century

Movement-under-load training is still used today, most extensively by the military in the form of rucking, which has gradually made its way to aspects of civilian athlete training. In boxing and wrestling training there is a long tradition of wearing ankle weights ala the Chippewa to add resistance to distance runs.

But let's look to the great Joe Louis for two ways, one standard and one less so, that he used to assist his long tenure as heavyweight champion of the world. The Brown Bomber did his "rock runs" (we will play with rock runs a bit later) in a pair of heavy boots. His trainers, Jack Blackburn and Mannie Seamon, made it a point to select heavy boots for roadwork. The heavier the better. Essentially footwear as ankle weights.

Another less expected practice to build sport specific resistance—a thicker than average padding beneath the canvas of Louis' training ring. Seamon regularly added 3/4 inch of padding to the standard padding depth so that Louis was working against resistance in both movement and power throughout his training. Seamon felt that when it came to fight night it gave the champ added snap to his punches and made his movement lighter, more akin to a middleweight. I can testify to a bit of that. I use a double layer of Reselite wrestling mats for training, and when stepping onto a single layer it feels absurdly fast.

There are many more examples from history, cultures and individual athletes of movement-under-load training, but the offered instances should give us a healthy respect for the practice. And perhaps cause us to consider adding these ideas to our own training giving it a bit of historical heft.

7. The Corbett jab

The primary facet that distinguishes Corbett's jab from a standard jab is the lack of fist turnover. If we hold our hands up in defensive position and have a look at our jabbing fist we will see that the palm is facing to the inside line, but not perfectly so. It has an ever-so-slight twist of the

Library of Congress

palm forward. When the standard jab is fired, the fist begins a thumb-to-the-inside-line rotation that ends with it making contact with the palm facing down. This twist and snapping drive is what powers many a good, strong jab puncher.

Corbett's jab never loses the onguard orientation. It arrives at its target as it left neutral—that is, with the fist striking just off-center of vertical. If we take this jab to the bag, to the pads or to the sparring ring we will find almost immediately that it lacks the oomph of a turnover jab executed with proper snap. But we do gain three unexpected attributes that I wager Corbett had in mind when facing his foes who were schooled in heavy hitting as opposed to finesse.

1. Speed of execution

Corbett's jab is not necessarily using the hip twist and other driving mechanics since it is primarily an arm punch, almost exclusively arm and shoulder driven. This use of less muscle and body mass to fire the punch results in less power, but in a bit more speed.

2. Perceptual speed

Since the punch lacks the need to make large body shifts, it is a harder read. Take it to the mirror and have a look for yourself. Throw standard jabs and watch for telegraphing. Even if you have a solid jab with few tells there is a bit of body English that goes into firing it. Now watch yourself throw Corbett's jab. You will find there are far less tells that signal punch intent.

3. The jab as foil defense

The arm of the jab fired in this position is a stop-hit tool. That is, a speedy counter that serves to disrupt attacks before they start or before they arrive. And if a punch is incoming while throwing the Corbett jab, we find that our arm behaves as a fencing foil—blocking/deflecting the incoming punch with no forward head-lean.

Again, not a powerful punch, but I sincerely think it was not designed to be so. It was designed to disrupt a powerful opponent. It was used to score points, while the rounds away and wear men down. It was used as a fencing probe to remain active and light on the feet without having to settle down into your punches. Then, when the time was right, one could shift to power punches including snapping the jab in the standard manner.

Gentleman Jim's jab

James "Gentleman Jim" Corbett is regularly acknowledged as the dividing line from the brawler-slugger era of the sport to the gloved and "scientific" era. This is easy shorthand for a more complex story. Corbett himself would tout the scientific method of fighting, which means more fluidity and the addition of finesse punches into the midst of the usual power arsenal.

> ...Corbett is regularly acknowledged as the dividing line from the brawler-slugger era of the sport to the gloved and "scientific" era.

"In the old days of the London prize ring there were hard and fast rules for training. Today they are to be laughed at. They may have been all right for those men in those days, but they would not do now. They did not look for speed then, but rather developed a physique that was oak-like in its strength, and cultivated a blow that would fell an ox — if it landed. Blows like that are too easily avoided nowadays, and the man who feints and sidesteps has to be reckoned with."

Corbett acknowledges heavy power, power that is to be avoided. This power avoidance was a hallmark of his style and part and parcel of what allowed him to render the seemingly impervious John L. Sullivan a bit, well, pervious.

Corbett was not a heavy hitter, but that lack of power seems to be more of a choice than lack of oomph. Out of 20 fights we see a mere five wins by knockout. If we recall Corbett's own words we can reason that he practiced what he preached—he made a point of using footwork, evasion, and movement in general to avoid power. He was working in an era where there was such an emphasis on power that he strategized running in the other direction would give him an advantage.

Adding to his chosen light hand was his jab form. He used the jab frequently and was, at the time, one of the best big men using the tool. But his choice of fist contact or striking position lessened its power. We can only surmise that a fighter as intelligent and well considered as Corbett knew that he was choosing a less than powerful jab and that choice was one made for speed—both speed of execution and perceptual speed.

Let's break down Corbett's jab, have a look at some of its positive attributes and then put it through some drill paces.

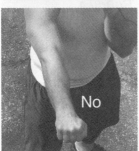

Five rounds of Corbett's flip-flop jabbing

An acknowledged light punch, the tool should not be a primary, but it has its place.

Round 1
Work the Corbett jab on the heavy bag or pads. Do not forget to apply it with light footwork, emphasizing the side step.

Round 2
Work your standard boxing on pads or bag, but return to using the standard jab.

Corbett jab.

43

Round 3
Work using the Corbett jab with a rear hand power follow up. It will initially feel odd to go light then HEAVY, but it will come.

Round 4
Work the standard jab and the Corbett jab in an alternating manner so that you can get used to changing the flavors inside a round or even inside a combination.

Corbett jab as a foil.

Round 5
Take it to pads or light sparring where your feeder/partner is playing the role of the bigger more powerful fighter and you must use the Corbett jab as intended. Stay on your bicycle, pepper the Corbett jab and if the opportunity for the power followup occurs, seize it. Again, not a powerful tool, but a canny and speedy tool that has its place.

8. "Attacking the buckler" from Heenan to Louis

First, what's a "buckler?" A buckler is a small, round shield wielded by swordsmen or spearmen. It is worn on the defensive forearm or held in the defensive hand. While the weapon hand went to work, the buckler was used to deflect blows and at times used as a weapon itself. OK, so what does a buckler have to do with boxing? In the early days of the sport, boxing was thought of as an auxiliary activity to other forms of combat. Early boxing academies were not purely establishments for boxing training. They often offered a myriad of disciplines that were taught in tandem with one another.

Encyclopædia Britannica, from *Pugilistica*

James Figg

There are numerous records of bouts where the participants not only boxed but also might engage in fencing, wrestling and singlestick matches (essentially sword dueling with a stout stick standing in for the sword itself). One of the anointed fathers of modern boxing, James Figg, was an accomplished swordsman and engaged in many singlestick duels.

As part and parcel with swordfighting we often see offensive and defensive buckler tactics. When the buckler was not in use the rear arm (defensive arm) was still held in the "buckler-ready" position. What is buckler-ready position? Assume your boxing stance. Now look at your rearward arm,

45

with its bent elbow and fist-up position. Congrats, you have now had your first sword and buckler lesson.

To distract, feint or open a line, swordsmen would often attack the buckler itself. There was a transfer of this tactic from swordplay to the empty-handed boxing scufflers who knew that the occasional "attacking of the naked buckler" could have its uses. There are myriad instances of attacking the buckler, but let's look at a mere two. One from the early era when swordplay, wrestling and singlestick were also part of the boxing curriculum. And one from the modern era to demonstrate that the tactic still has a good deal to recommend it.

Frank Leslie, public domain

John Camel Heenan

John Camel Heenan, the "Benicia Boy," was an American prize fighter who decided to cross the pond and take on the British champion, Tom Sayers. The two met on April 17, 1860. The fight ended in absolute chaos when the crowd rushed the ring after Heenan tried to "strangle" Sayers by pushing his head down and across the ropes in the 37th round. After this melee, the ring was set up a short distance away and the much battered and bruised warriors recommenced for five more rounds before the police were spotted and the crowd dispersed (prizefighting being illegal at this time).

Both men gave and received a good deal of punishment, but contemporary reports have it that Sayers was looking supe-

Attacking the buckler.

rior with good defense when by either luck or design Heenan attacked the buckler. Heenan, having trouble penetrating Sayers defense, launched heavy blows at the defense itself and in the 6th one of these did the trick rendering Sayers right arm quite useless.

Heenan's eye was closed in the 7th and yet these men carried on for 42 rounds and over two hours of brutal punishment. So, here we have an instance of banging the arms (attacking the buckler) to gain advantage.

Let's look to a 20th century example—Joe Louis (yeah, Joe again, but when the well is deep, drink deep). Joe is facing the very slick Lee Ramage for his first time. The two met for this inaugural bout in Chicago, December 10, 1934. Joe is having trouble penetrating Ramage's tight defense. He heads back to his corner after the sixth round and says, "I can't get a good shot at him." To which, the ever wise Jack Blackburn replies, "Well, he's got arms ain't he?" The canny Mr. Blackburn told the Brown Bomber to attack the buckler. By the eighth round Ramage had trouble holding his arms up and Joe put him away.

Six rounds of attacking the buckler

Round 1

Get on the heavy bag and either visualize the arms in defensive position or chalk "arms" onto the bag for precise targeting. Go to work banging hard and heavy hooks to the biceps and forearms.

Round 2

Stay on the heavy bag. Work taking slide steps to the inside and outside lines while placing straight punches to the arms (buckler).

Round 3

Work on combining the arm hooking and sliding straights.

Round 4

Grab your sparring partner and each take turns being a shelled up, cautious fighter. Work the arm hooks with control so you both can keep playing.

Round 5

Now, work the sliding straights to the buckler with your partner.

Round 6

Combine the hooks and straights and your other boxing tactics. With this minor change in targeting and the six preceding drills, we can go a long way from seeing a shelled up, good defense to seeing everything (and I mean everything) as a target.

9. Frank Moran's "Mary Ann"

Frank Moran was saddled with the less than glamourous ring name of "The Fighting Dentist." He studied dentistry for three years at the University of Pittsburgh, hence the name, but if we take a look at that big right hand of his there is no doubt that many a jaw that received it might have been in need of the profession.

Library of Congress

Frank Moran (let) with Jess Willard.

Moran was fighting in the unfortunate era of the search for the "Great White Hope" when a vociferous lot were rabidly clamoring to dethrone the "uppity" black champion, Jack Johnson. Moran was to face Johnson and stay on his feet for the full twenty rounds. Not only did he stay on his feet he won more than a few rounds and to some eyes the decision should have been his. The referee, and "White Hope" himself, Georges Carpentier, handed the decision to Johnson. Watch the fight for yourself and make your own decision.

Moran was to go on for a second shot at the heavyweight crown when he took on the man who dethroned Johnson, Jess Willard. Willard, who stood six foot, five inches and never weighed less than 225 pounds (often far above), towered over Moran who never tipped the scales higher than

206. Moran lasted the entire ten-round distance of this fight with the result going to the champion. Ringside reports have it that this decision was the correct one.

What we can gather from these two showings, plus many more, was that Moran was durable and had skills—but his single best weapon was that big right hand that he named Mary Ann. Let's take a look at how he was throwing it to snag a bit of that power that kept bigger and, some say, better men on the wise side of wary.

Five rounds to woo Mary Ann

Round 1
On the heavy bag, stand in good position and throw strong, solid rear straights. Reset each time and find maximum power.

Round 2
Now let's lay back in our stance a little bit.
● Moran would ride a little tall and over the rear foot with around an 80/20 weight distribution favoring this rear foot.
● The extra distance allows more travel in the rear straight.
● Back on the bag and fire.

Round 3
Now let's put that rear leg to work as Moran did.
● Start the rear straight with a flex of the calf, not a hip-shift. Let this flex propel toes on the canvas to get the drive going.
● As the punch is turning to make impact, lock that rear leg and snap that hip at the moment of impact.
● Back on the bag to work the kinks out.

Round 4
Here's where it gets a little hairy. Moran would dip his head, seemingly bad form and a prize for a good uppercut. But with good lead-hand coverage or an accompanying muffle, we put this powerful shot back on the viable table.
● As you fire the shot, rather than keep your head in standard position, chin down and eyes up….

● Moran would dip the head more so the ear is practically on the deltoid of the extended rear straight.

● This head-down, ear-in position seems to add a bit of inertia and weight commitment providing Mary Ann with her power.

Round 5
Run a standard blowout round on the bag, but emphasize rear straights in your combinations and make them all Mary Anns.

Mr. Moran may have never captured the heavyweight title, but he faced two esteemed champs and many a fine contender and all of them had respect for that big punch with the sweet name.

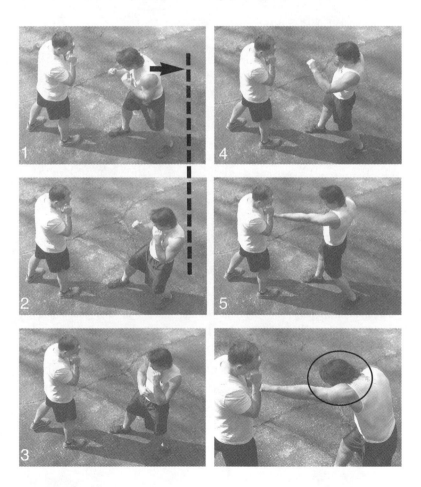

10. "Gunboat" Smith's "occipital punch"

First, let's get that ring name out of the way. In the days of intriguing, but not always martial ring names, Ed Smith (formerly Ed Eckblad or Eckhad, depending on which reference you use) was saddled with the appellation "Gunboat." He says this came about from his stint in the Navy when a fellow sailor aboard the U.S.S. Pennsylvania remarked on the size of his feet and that it would take shoes the size of gunboats to shod him. For the record, his shoe size was 11, which may not strike today's readers as all that gunboaty.

"GUNBOAT" SMITH.

Library of Congress

In a 90-fight career, Gunboat accrued 52 wins—38 by knockout. If we factor in all of his fights, draws included, he has a KO percentage of 42 percent. Mighty respectable.

We include Mr. Smith in this gallery of champs, although he was not a champ for two reasons and a suspect third. The first reason—he fought Dempsey twice. The second fight was something of a one-sided affair, some ringside reporters called it a "slaughter" with Gunboat hitting the canvas seven times in two rounds (some said nine drops.) But in that first bout Mr. Smith gave Mr. Dempsey a mighty big run for his money. It was only a four-round affair with the decision going to Dempsey, but Dempsey could not put him away and Gunboat rocked the Mauler hard in the 3rd. More on that in a bit.

Let's look at the suspect third reason Mr. Smith is in these pages. On October 11th, 1909, Smith faced Jack Johnson in a four-round exhibition. More than a few newspapers across the country reported that Smith dropped Johnson two minutes into the 4th round and Johnson had to be "saved" by his managers by cutting the match short. Keep in mind, the exhibition took placed in San Francisco and the local newspaper reporting the matches that day, *The San Francisco Call,* makes no mention of the incident. They state that Johnson faced Smith, but that is it.

This occurred during the racist search for "The Great White Hope" and it is not beyond the realm of possibility that the story was manufactured to appease bigoted opinion. Even if we minus out the possibly false Johnson droppage and his second bout with Dempsey, we are left with stories of a man with a MEAN right hand. That right hand is the reason we want to spend some time with Gunboat.

Gunboat threw a rear overhand that came to be known as the "occipital punch." The occipital portion of the skull is the back of the head. With that in mind, we are taking a hard look at a blow that is illegal in today's game, but for a bit of historical recreational activity let's have a look at how Gunboat gave Dempsey so much trouble that first time.

Six rounds to the occipital punch

Round 1

Get in front of your bag, a tear-drop bag or uppercut bag is ideal for this one, but it can still be worked on a standard heavy bag. Throw a standard rear overhand.

● Allow the punch to launch as if starting a rear straight.

● As it leaves the shoulder allow the fist to travel an upward arc and then…

● Slam downward into the face, neck or shoulder.

● Picture holding a baseball in the rear hand and I have demanded that you throw that ball into the core of the earth come hell or high water and you give it all the wind-up you can.

Round 2

Repeat the prior round, but this time add a step with the lead foot to the outside. The step provides both more "oomph!" and a better angle to land.

Round 3

For this round, let's tweak our arcing angle.

● Rather than chopping that overhand up and down…

● Allow it to cheat towards the outside of the throwing arm.

● Think of it as a bit of a loooong loose hook.
● Again, the outside step will allow the angle to feel a bit more natural.

Round 4

For this round we will alter the striking surface a bit.
● Rather than the face of the glove making first contact...
● Think of the bottom of the fist towards the palm, or even the bottom inside of the wrist making contact.

Round 5

Now let's use that outside step to cheat forward to alter our target.
● Keep your outside step, but...
● Increase the forward drive as if we are going to over-shoot our punching target.
● We are throwing over and past the shoulder rather than any line along the shoulder.

Round 6

Now we'll put it all together.
● As your modified overhand loops over the shoulder and lands with the modified striking surface…
● Whip that striking surface back towards yourself.
● Use the punching biceps to retract/whip the fist towards yourself at the last moment.
● Think of gorilla thumping your chest hard at the moment of impact.

I think by simply reading the description before you take it to the bags you can see why Gunboat's occipital punch carried such a wallop.

Hell, if it could rattle Dempsey, it can rattle anyone.

11. Kid Gavilan's bolo punch

Gerardo Gonzalez, better known in the ring as Kid Gavilan, also carried the nom de ring of "The Cuban Hawk." We'll stick with Kid Gavilan or Kid for this lesson.

The Kid was a mighty slick boxer who held the welterweight crown from 1952 to 1954. Let's focus on one aspect of the Kid's slickness, a punch that has become synonymous with his name—the bolo punch. The bolo itself in various names and guises has been around since man has doubled fist and thrown hands at one another. Gavilan himself is not necessarily the first to throw it under the name "bolo." That distinction belongs to Ceferino Garcia, the winningest fighter of Filipino descent and holder of the middleweight title for a time. As early as 1924 Garcia is reported as using a punch called the bolo, which is a Filipino dialect word for "machete."

> The bolo punch is not the flourish...but the punch itself.

Again, Gavilan wasn't the first, nor was Garcia—they were the men who brought it to fore under that name. Nor were they the last to use it. Sugar Ray Leonard and Pedro Carrasco were fine bolo punchers themselves. The bolo is usually thought of for the flourish that the Kid would use preceding it, but that is a bit of a red herring. The bolo punch is not the flourish which may or may not precede it, but the punch itself. For a devasting look at a non-flourish use of the bolo have a look at Ike Ibeabuchi's KO of Chris Byrd in their 1999 bout. Ouch!

Lead bolo with a machete   Lead bolo sans flourish.

Twelve rounds to the bolo punch
Round 1
First, we'll build the basic motion. Grab a stick (or a machete!), say 18 inches long. Hold it in your lead hand and start swinging it in tight underhand, upward arcing circles. Swing from the elbow and not the shoulder.

Round 2
Repeat with the rear hand.

Round 3
Repeat the lead without the stick.

Round 4
Repeat round two without the stick.

Round 5
Now for the bolo punch sans implement. Let's start with the lead hand.
● Think of splitting the difference between a hook and an uppercut, but thrown at a loose angle. This is not a shovel hook, which is tighter to the body.
● Target the jaw, with orthodox fighters seeing the fist travel from 7 o'clock on the clockface straight to the 2 position.
● Unorthodox fighters will travel the fist from 4 across the clock to 10.

Round 6
Repeat with the rear hand.
● Orthodox fighters will travel across the clockface 4 to 10.
● Southpaws 7 to 2.

Rear flourish, lead bolo.

Lead flourish, rear bolo.

Round 7
Rear hand flourish to lead bolo.

Round 8
Lead hand flourish to rear bolo.

Round 9
Lead flourish to lead bolo.

Round 10
Rear flourish to rear bolo.

Round 11
Counter the jab with a lead non-flourish bolo. Feel free to use a jab catch or pat for safety.

Lead flourish, lead bolo.

Rear flourish, rear bolo.

Round 12
Counter a rear straight with a rear non-flourish bolo. Slipping outside with a check hand in play is wise.

Like most worthy endeavors, the devil is in the details and adding this split-angle beauty can provide plenty of devilish details to harry your opponent.

Counter jab with lead bolo, no flourish.

12. George Dawson & the kidney punch

First things first—do NOT fire kidney punches in the sport. I include this now illegal tactic for a bit of historical delving. What happens in a self-defense or street application is a horse of another color.

> Firing shots to the kidneys has likely been a feature of armed and unarmed combat since man began walloping one another.

Firing shots to the kidneys has likely been a feature of armed and unarmed combat since man began walloping one another. Just when the name "kidney punch" became a separate idea in the early era of boxing is a bit unclear, but legend ballparks it on an early lightweight champion of the bareknuckle era — George Dawson.

Dawson was born on October 7, 1867 in New South Wales, Australia. His town of nativity went by the colorful name Dark Corner. His parents had emigrated from England during the Australian Gold Rush. There is not much known about Dawson's early years beyond that he was encouraged to try the sport after the death of his parents. He was rather active on the Australian scene during the 1880s and early 1890s. He boxed over 292 rounds in his career. Included in some of those rounds was time spent against Bob Fitzsimmons and Tommy Ryan.

In the course of his career he picked up the lightweight crown of Queensland in 1887 and he held the lightweight title of Australia from 1889-1891. Dawson was dubbed the inventor of the kidney punch, but this designation seems to come long after his career was over. An article from the mid-1930s (perhaps 1935) titled "The Boxer and Wrestler" declares Dawson the inventor. Unlikely he was the inventor, but indications are good that his reputation for using it was well deserved. Let's have a look at a few applications of this mighty painful blow.

First, the target area. Assuming nothing, let's find the general area that is so much of the problem. Reach behind you with either hand and feel for the soft patch of skin beneath your ribs and above your hipbone. This tender spot on your back about three inches away from your spine is the target area.

One can already see that with the target being on the back this was most likely off limits in most "fair play" bouts. But beyond accidental kidney punches and/or an opponent who runs (blatantly turns their back), there are a few sneaky ways to get this blow in.

Eleven rounds to kidney punching prowess

Round 1

Side step and dig.

● Take a big outside step with the rear foot—even better if we make that side step 45 degrees and forward.

● Throw a loose rear hook to the target.

● As it rounds the torso, use the biceps to snap the punch into the target.

● You will not have a clean shot at the kidneys without this snap, so keep that snap a constant.

Round 2

Repeat with the lead hand.

● Take that big sliding step forward and to the outside.

● Snap that fist into the target.

Side step and dig, rear hand.

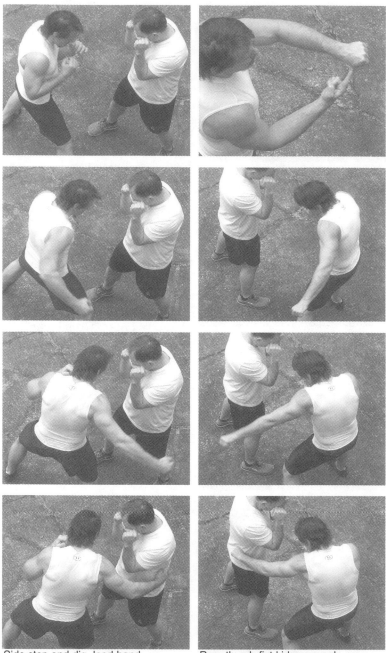

Side step and dig, lead hand.   Rear thumb-fist kidney punch

Round 3
Rear thumb-fist kidney punch.
● You can deliver this blow gloved or ungloved. It is similar to Battling Nelson's dig to the liver.
● Keep all of your mechanics including the step and snap, but here…
● Make impact with the thumb side of the fist. The soft target area makes injuring the hand unlikely and the biceps snap feels a bit stronger with the hand in this position.

Round 4
Lead thumb-fist kidney punch.
● Repeat round two with the thumb fist.

Lead thumb-fist kidney punch

Lead cupping kidney shot

Rear cupping kidney shot

Round 5

Rear cupping kidney shot.
● This sneaky little tool from the bareknuckle era provides a surprising percussive wallop.
● Make a cup with your ungloved hand as you would to bring water to your mouth from a mountain stream.
● Use all of the round 1 mechanics and allow this cupping hand to apply a percussive snap to the target.

Round 6

Lead cupping kidney shot

Clinch cupping kidney punch

Round 7

The preceding blows are a bit blatant, but the following allows us to hide the intent.

● As your opponent steps in with a long jab, hit any of the preceding tactics.

● Timing the shot with your opponent's incoming movement gives the appearance of an accidental shot that overshot the "intended" legal target.

Round 8

Let's look at hiding it off a rear straight from your opponent.

● If a lunging rear straight is fired, side step 45 degrees to the outside and forward and dig the shot using your opponent's lunge as the "hide."

Round 9

Clinch kidney punch.

● The punch is easily fired here. It is easily read, but for historical or street sake...

● On the bag, work clinching and snapping the punch to the kidney area.

Round 10

Clinch thumb fist.

● Repeat the bag drill, but here use the thumb-fist to make impact.

Round 11

Clinch cupping kidney shot.

● On the bag. You know what to do. Again, illegal in today's game, questionable in the early days, but mighty effective.

Library of Congress

13. Champ to champ

Grantland Rice, "Granny" to those who knew the man, was one of the premier sports writers of the 20th century. If there were giants in the game, any game, he wrote about them, he spent time with them, and chances are he supped and imbibed with them. He covered the fight game from the end of World War I right up until his death at the age of 73 on July 13, 1954. He died at his typewriter in a poetic bit of fate for a legendary newspaperman.

Here's Granny on Jack Dempsey.

"Dempsey was the oddest mixture of humanity I've known. In the ring he was a killer—a superhuman wild man. His teeth were frequently bared and his complete intent was an opponent's destruction. He was a fighter—one who used every trick to wreck the other fighter.

"Yet, outside the ring, Jack is one of the gentlest men I know. I've seen him in his restaurant at times when some customer, with more enthusiasm than good sense, would grab his vest or part of his shirt—strictly for a souvenir—with no kickback from Jack. I've known the man closely for more than thirty years and I've never seen him in a rough argument or anything except courteous and considerate."

One can make an argument for the strong moral lesson from a great champ: One can be a fighter and still be a laid-back gentleman. It is not necessary to be "ready to rumble" in all encounters. If Jack Dempsey could keep his cool, surely many other lesser lights could do the same in minor disagreements outside the ring.

But we're here to talk fighting, tactics, old school fistic wisdom. Let's go back to Granny and an incident from 1931.

"I was having breakfast with Jack and Max Baer one February morning back in 1931 at the Warwick Hotel. The day before, Jack had refereed the Max Baer/Tommy [Lefty] Loughran fight at Madison Square Garden. Max had been decisioned in ten rounds.

Library of Congress

" 'I've been looking at left jabs all night,' Max said. 'Lefts…lefts… lefts…that's all I've seen!'

" 'The funny part,' said Dempsey, 'is that you could have stopped Lefty in the first round.'

" 'How?' said Baer.

" 'Take off your coat,' replied Jack to big Maxie, 6 feet 3 and 220 pounds. Max shucked off his coat and faced Dempsey.

" 'Now lead with a left, just as Loughran did,' said Jack. Max led…and there was [an] immediate yelp. 'You broke my arm,' Max howled as he backed away, holding it.

"As Baer led with his left, Dempsey had dropped his huge right fist across the left biceps with paralyzing force. The left arm became useless for thirty minutes."

According to Granny, Dempsey used a variation of Jack Johnson's biceps punch. Let's move from the story to the how-to.

Lead hook biceps chop.

Rear hook biceps chop.

Ten rounds to Dempsey's paralyzer defense

Round 1

● Get in front of a heavy bag and envision an incoming jab. Use the lead hand to chop inward and down at a 45-degree angle into the biceps of the incoming punching arm.

● Make the movement short and choppy so that you don't pull your defense or followups out of position.

● Where Johnson would apply very little force to his biceps punch, Dempsey, being Dempsey, would put some "falling step" muscle into the shot to give it more immediate bite.

Round 2

Repeat the bag drill envisioning an incoming rear straight. Use the rear hand for the chop.

Round 3

Stay on the bag and envision a lead hook incoming. Use the same chop mechanics but with a bit more outward travel.

Lead uppercut biceps chop.

Rear uppercut biceps chop.

Round 4
Repeat the protocol with incoming rear hooks.

Round 5
Envision an uppercut (lead or rear) and use the lead hand to down chop the biceps. Think short, choppy, explosive.

Round 6
Stay with envisioning uppercuts, but here use the rear hand to chop.

Round 7
Grab a partner and, with care, pick off jabs and rear straights.

Round 8
Repeat the partner round with lead and rear hooks as the feed.

Round 9
Now let's bite those uppercuts.

Round 10
Take care of your partner while they feed all angles and you spend the round chopping them all. It is wise to take all of these partner rounds at half speed. One good paralyzer, let alone several, will do your partner in for the day.

14. Jack Slack's "chopper"

Here's an oldie but goldie from the historical record—the chopper. Helluva name, huh? Is it legal? Not any more, but there was a time when one of our early champs used it to square up his otherwise finesse-less game. Being illegal now, it is one for historical recreation or a bit of fist-saving street defense.

> His ring name? The Norfolk Butcher. A bit obvious, but also pretty badass.

Jack Slack was a butcher from Norfolk in the east of England. His ring name? The Norfolk Butcher. A bit obvious, but also pretty badass. Mr. Slack was a powerful man, standing no more than five foot eight or nine, but tipping the scales in the 200 pounds range. He built his physique hefting sides of beef and swinging a heavy cleaver.

When Slack began taking to the ring in 1743, he started a walk through local champions that led to him eventually being crowned champion of England after defeating the legendry (and likely more talented) Jack Broughton on April 11, 1750. There is no contemporary report that declares Mr. Slack was grace in motion, or that he floated like a butterfly and stung like an 18th-century bee. Most all accounts report him as a clumsy or "lubberly" fighter and yet he did pretty damn well for a grounded non-bee.

Beyond being the man to defeat Jack Broughton, his fame resides in a particular tactic, one that he did not use often, but when he did it seemed to do the trick. This tactic was a curious backhand punch that he called the chopper (one of the all-time best tactic names). The chopper was a variant of a bottom fist or hammer fist maneuver. What made it different was Slack's muscular way of doling it out and his unusual method for winding it up.

Jack Slack (right) defeated Jack Broughton to become champion of England in 1750. It was said a hard shot to an eye blinded Broughton to Slack's subsequent assault.

Covering up.

Lunge, unwind, backhand strike.

Four rounds to Jack Slack's chopper

Round 1

Fold both arms before you as if in a deep Philly cover. Contemporary descriptions have it that Mr. Slack went so far as to have his fists touch his chest. He would also bury that head a bit behind this barricade of bone.

Round 2

Lunge

● The blow was not delivered from stance or a static position, so like all good heavy punches it was accompanied by a forceful lunge step to assist the unwinding from this initially awkward position.

Round 3

Single

● Hit your lunge step. As your lead foot hits the canvas unwind the top arm (the lead arm) and twisting from the waist...

● Forcefully make contact with the bottom fist or outside of wrlst/forearm.

● Time the blow to match the planting of the lunge step.

● When throwing the single, the rear hand pulls to standard safety next to the rear cheek.

Lunge, unwind, backhand, rear hand.

Round 4

Double

● This is where it gets really interesting in my opinion.

● Mr. Slack often threw the chopper as a paired blow.

● He would lunge step and unwind with all the mechanics of the single. Rather than pull the rear arm to the cheek...

● He would allow the torso twist of the first chopper to wind his waist towards the lead side, which loads the rear chopper...

● And immediately unloads with the opposite hand.

Once you give this one a few rounds of play I think you'll gain a newfound respect for this ungainly double blow. It possesses surprising wallop and in all ring tests, if used sparingly, it is mighty surprising—hard to see coming and at least one of the twin choppers always finds it's mark.

15. Building Dempsey's hook

We all know Jack Dempsey had power in those hands. His two fists of dynamite are the stuff of boxing legend. But according to his trainer Jimmy DeForest he didn't start out that way. DeForest thought he was tough, a good worker, but what impressed him most was his legs. The power from the hips down. While he was impressed with his power, he was less impressed with his mobility. (We'll get to how he addressed that deficiency in an upcoming chapter.) He felt that Dempsey wasn't getting all he could out of his hands power-wise (almost hard to believe), so he remedied the problem thusly:

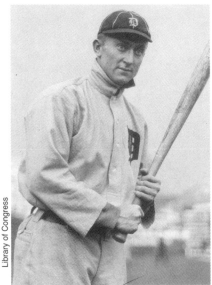

Ty Cobb and Jack Dempsey shared a tip.

"There are also some tales to the effect that great left hook was made by strapping his right hand to his side and making him use only the southpaw in practice. That's wrong, too. What I did was put an iron weight in his left glove and made him work from a half to three-quarters of an hour each day pounding the bag.

"The principle is the same as Ty Cobb discovered in swinging four bats while waiting his turn at the plate. When he finally faced the pitcher, that one bat seemed light and easy to handle. When the weight was taken out of his glove, Dempsey experienced the same sensation."

We're going to borrow from DeForest *and* Ty Cobb to build some Dempsey power.

Six rounds to Dempsey/Cobb power

Admittedly six rounds does not get us to the 30 to 45 minutes DeForest advises, but one can simply double the offered drill circuit and get in the DeForest ballpark.

Ty Cobb shadowboxing
● Grab some 10-15 pound dumbbells and spend three rounds working your hooks and uppercuts.
● We want to build power but don't swing/sling hard and fast as the inertia of the weight will start stealing your form. You will begin to build power by mere dint of hefting the heavy weight through the proper motions.

Dempsey bag work
● Don some loaded gloves, one pound minimum and no more than two pounds. We don't want to injure our hands.
● Spend three rounds up to speed, banging like Luis Firpo is about to bull you out of the ring.

I recommend these two in tandem and the order offered. The Ty Cobb rounds will allow a bit of fatigue to accrue, but dropping the weight from say 15-pound dumbbells to 2-pound loaded gloves will feel like a snap. Inverting the order pays fewer dividends. Swing like Cobb! Bang like Dempsey!

16. "Hurricane" Jackson's "scoop punch"

Tommy Jackson was one of those terrific fighters that never quite gained a belt. He was in the mix at the top ranks, but that final step to the top was just out of reach. In 1955 he outpointed former heavyweight champion Ezzard Charles twice and earned a shot in the elimination tournament to fill Rocky Marciano's vacancy in 1956. He lost a twelve-round decision in that tournament to Floyd Patterson.

> Bimstein said, "The kid is like the old-timers in his training. Nothing is too much or too hard for him to do..."

He was thought of highly enough to become Patterson's first title defense in 1957, but lost to a TKO. Legendary trainer Whitey Bimstein thought so much of him that he added him to his stable, and Bimstein knew talent. Lest we forget, Bimstein played a hand in the careers of some of the best there ever was including Jack Dempsey, Gene Tunney, Harry Greb, Benny Leonard, Billy Conn, two Rockys (Graziano and Marciano) and many others. At one point in the 1930s every single weight class champion was of Bimstein stock. With that said, if Bimstein thought a good deal of Tommy Jackson, it's safe to say so should we.

Jackson had a frenetic whirlwind style (hence the ring name "Hurricane") that Bimstein put on par with Harry Greb and

Henry Armstrong. He was noted for his fantastic conditioning and imperviousness to punishment.

Regarding his training Bimstein said, "The kid is like the old-timers in his training. Nothing is too much or too hard for him to do. Ask him to run two miles and he wants to jog twelve." Freddie Brown, Bimstein's partner in the enterprise, stated that he and Bimstein "had to argue with Jackson to keep him from overtraining."

This fantastic conditioning underlies much of Jackson's style and is likely what allowed him to get away with an unusual feature of his arsenal that Whitey Bimstein called his "scoop punch." The scoop punch is basically a double uppercut and it manifested in a few different ways. Let's get off the page and take it to the gym and put it to work.

Lead and rear uppercuts—BAM! BAM!

Lead and rear uppercuts to the chin.

Seven rounds to "Hurricane" Jackson's scoop punch

Round 1

The first version of the scoop is more of a single uppercut with a second one following right on the heels of the first.

● Belly up to the bag and fire a lead uppercut to the midsection and then a rear uppercut right behind it.

● Time it so that we hear the impact as an extremely quick combination—BAM! BAM!

Round 2

Repeat the lower uppercuts, but this time fire the rear uppercut first.

Round 3

Let's go back to firing the lead uppercut first, but let's fire these twins to the chin.

Round 4

Repeat with the rear hand firing first.

Scoop to the midsection.

Round 5
Here's where Jackson really breaks the rule. You will fire the uppercuts simultaneously while touching the gloves together as one solid fist.
● For this round let's fire the scoop to the midsection.

Round 6
For this round scoop to the chin.

Round 7
Now take it out of isolation.
● Bang the bag hard and pepper with your personal mix of blows, but work mixing in the rapid fire scoops and actual scoops here and there.

Chances are the rapid fire scoops won't feel too bad, but the actual two-fisted scoop punch will initially feel a bit awkward. It requires time and, to be honest, more than a bit of that Hurricane Jackson work ethic to put it across.

Scoop to the chin.

17. Smokin' Joe's erratic bob & weave

Smokin' Joe Frazier is one of those legends so indelibly carved in memory and of recent enough vintage that it hardly seems necessary to introduce or remind the even semi-knowledgeable of who he was and why he is still so GD influential. His work ethic was formidable. His demeanor during work tells the other half of a story that is not mere "He puts the training time in." Mr. Frazier tells the tale:

> "Your body is going forward, but your head, you gotta make it erratic."
>
> —Eddie Futch

"You can map out a fight plan or a life plan, but when the action starts, it may not go the way you planned, and you're down to your reflexes—that means your [preparation]. That's where your roadwork shows. If you cheated on that in the dark of the morning, well, you're going to get found out now, under the bright lights."

Joe worked. Worked hard. Dial up Joe in his early years and you see that work pay off inside the ring. Watch the almost tireless upper-body movement. That amount and degree of evasive upper-body work requires a vast reservoir of energy.

If you doubt it, try this:
- Stand up, right now.
- Start bobbing and weaving, juking and jiving.
- Keep it up for one solid minute. No more, no less.
- Put some pep in it, don't just go through the motions.
- Once you've completed, listen to your breathing.

Are you sucking wind through your mouth?

Not Joe. Joe worked this hard round after round and still kept good jaw-saving, mouth-closed discipline. The other remarkable thing about Joe's upper-body evasion is its seemingly erratic quality. That is not chaotic happenstance, that is educated chaos. And it is a chaos that came later in his game than one may first assume which shows that this great champion was always willing to evolve.

Frazier was a 1964 Gold Medal winning Olympian before turning pro. In his early days, Joe had that work ethic, but his style was more straight ahead. He looked mighty good in his first eleven pro fights, but number twelve was against Oscar Bonavena and Mr. Bonavena exploited Frazier's then straight-ahead style and had him on the canvas twice.

According to trainer Eddie Futch, a third time would have spelled the end. He told manager Yank Durham, "Yank, we've got to make this kid bob and weave because he can't walk in standing up straight like he's doing now." So Futch "...put a rope from one of the ring posts to the other, and...made him bob and weave under the rope."

Got it? We've all seen this drill. We may have even tried it on for size ourselves, but did we do it in Smokin' Joe fashion? Futch again:

"I taught him how to do it so that he wasn't in rhythm. I said, you see that speed bag? As long as it's coming right straight back to you, you can close your eyes all night long and hit it. But if it wobbles a little bit, then you have to hesitate to find where it's coming from. I want your head to do that. And never let the man know which way you're coming. Your body is going forward, but your head, you gotta make it erratic. Make it a little erratic."

According to Futch, erratic bobbing and weaving not only made Joe's head hard to find, what blows that did land did not land cleanly. "A lot of punches slid off his head where before they were glancing blows—because of the way his head was bobbing."

Twelve-plus rounds to Smokin' Joe's educated chaos

First things first...
● String your horizontal rope. About ear height should do it.
● With each drill iteration you will spend one round taking a single step, hit the iteration.
● Take another step, repeat the iteration.
● So on and so forth until you have burned all of your rounds stepping and putting that upper body through the paces.

Drill key
R = Moving right under the rope.
L = Moving left under the rope.

Thus, if you see RR, that will be two bobs under the rope. The first a true bob and weave to the right, the second a false return left, but reverse and bob back up to the right. Again, if you want to seize Joe's work ethic, you will spend at least one round on each.

Drill patterns
RLRL
LRLR
RRRR
LLLL
RRLR
LLRL
RLRR
LRLL
RRLL
LLRR
RLLR
LRRL

Stepping (forward) and bobbing.

Combining patterns

You can take these into the stratosphere by linking drill patterns as in the following examples:

RLRL RLLR

RLLL RLRL

The first twelve drills get you going and likely may be all you need, but if you've got a Smokin' Joe size heart you may combine and recombine to your heart's content.

18. Punching up, Marciano style

Rocco Francis Marchegiano. Let that name roll over your tongue. Savor it. Whether you call him by his birth name or the better known Rocky Marciano, that savor, that flavor is the distinct taste of undefeated legend.

49 Fights.
49 Wins.
43 Kos.
Losses, get outta here.

> "...he would get down like in a deep knee dip...start punching on the way up then wind up with a whomp—you know a big punch at the end of it. It's a difficult thing to do."
>
> —Angelo Dundee

This lesson is all about The Rock, but let's be honest, it's tough to pick up usable tips and tactics from this unique specimen because he was an awkward fighter. Never pretty. Never stylish. Never one of finesse.

Strong? Oh, yeah. Effective? The record speaks for itself.

But most all can view Marciano's fights and see we are looking at something that hews closer to the brawl side of things than the sweet side of boxing science. But if we dig a little deeper, we find some powerful gold. What Marciano had was strength, power, work ethic and, not commonly discussed, good balance.

When trainer Charley Goldman took on Marciano, he used his "Be you but more so" dictum and sought to make Rocky even Rockier. He sought to put that good balance, that power, that strength, and that stamina to good use. One fascinatingly useful tactic they decided on was "To Punch Up."

Let's let another legendary trainer, Angelo Dundee, tell the story of how Charley Goldman added sticks of dynamite to Rocky's power.

"He taught him [to] punch on the way up. I watched it. It was a heckuva move on the heavy bag. In other words, he would get down like in a deep knee dip, you know, straight down and start punching on the way up then wind up with a whomp—you know a big punch at the end of it. It's a difficult thing to do."

Difficult indeed, but doable with work ethic, which the Rock had.

Floor work & four starter rounds to Rocky's punching up

First, we need to add to our conditioning floor work to get the legs and lungs ready for the stamina required for good punching up.

Knee dips / knee-bends / Hindu squats
● It matters not what you want to call this exercise, but this has been used by combat athletes since man started fighting each other competitively to build stamina.
● In low numbers squats are a piece of cake, but a moderate number at a good clip gets the lungs pumping and the legs burning.
● Stand with feet slightly wider than shoulders.
● Toes facing forward or just slightly to the outside—slightly.
● Drop as low as you can remaining flat footed.
● It is best to allow the butt to drop backward so that the knees don't travel forward over the toes.

● At the bottom of the motion rise back to standing.
● That's one rep.
● Try knocking out 100 of these in a row at the start of each "Punch Up" session.

Now, let's go to the heavy bag.

Round 1
● Crouch and then explosively rise to fire a lead uppercut. Time the uppercut to impact on the rising extension.
● Crouch and repeat for the rear uppercut.
● Continue alternating looking for your timing and power.

Round 2
● Crouch and rise with a slight turn to the inside as you fire a lead hook. Again, look to time the impact with the rise-extension.
● Crouch and repeat with the rear hook.

Round 3
● Let's put this through the paces with the lead shovel hook. For the uninitiated, the shovel hook splits the difference between an uppercut and a hook, it travels at an angle as if throwing a shovel full of dirt over the opposite shoulder.
● Repeat with the rear shovel hook.

Round 4
● Mix 'em all up in your bag work. Once you find your timing and the bag dents admirably, you'll have a mean tool ready to unleash with every dip of the knee.

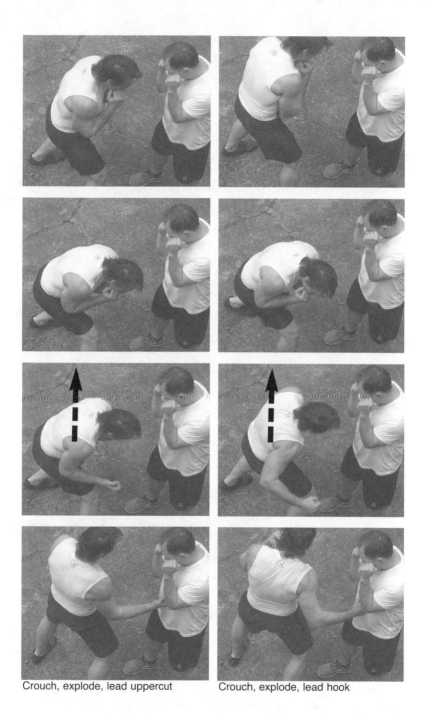

Crouch, explode, lead uppercut   Crouch, explode, lead hook

Shovel hooks follow a track midway between an uppercut and a hook.

Crouch, explode, lead shovel hook

19. Jack McCarthy's "chin hook" clinch

This lesson is not from a champ. Nor is the "chin hook" an actual punch per se.

Let's set the stage.

Heavyweight champion, Max Baer, wasn't champ for very long. His fun loving, playboy habits often got in the way of diligent training and his propensity for clowning showmanship, on occasion, cost him ground in the midst of tough battles. What was never in question was Bear's punching power, particularly that right hand. *The Ring* magazine rates him #22 in the "100 Greatest Punchers of All-Time," and he had the unfortunate specter of two ring deaths tagged to his name. Max had power even if he didn't always use it.

This lesson comes from an early Baer match in which he lost (on a DQ). So why do we do we include it here? His opponent in the bout in question was Jack McCarthy, a bit of a journeyman fighter, but undeniably tough. Mr. McCarthy had a method of controlling the clinch and delivering punishment that has been used by many fighters, but an observation from boxing journalist Jack Kofoed writing in 1934 allows us particular insight into how this clinch control was achieved. Kofoed writes, "Jack had a trick of getting in close, and laying his chin on the other fellow's shoulder and hammering away at the body with wild abandon."

This chin hook clinch, in essence, froze an opponent for a brief moment and allowed McCarthy to get off a few ripping shots to the body that the chin-hooked opponent had to absorb more than usual due to the freezing and hooking aspect of the ploy. The tactic served McCarthy well in his career, but Baer loved this sort of stockyard brawl and got in on the act until the referee disqualified Baer for a blow that drifted too far south.

Four rounds to the chin hook clinch

This one simply has to have a training partner to work well as bags don't have a correlating shoulder shelf to chin hook onto.

Round 1

Have your feeder don a body protector and pads. For the first round simply work a few punches from the outside, say a jab/cross to lead hook and respond to a fed jab by rocking away and following inside to a clinch. Strive for the chin hook. Lock the chin and hook downward as if to freeze the opponent flat-footed. Fire no body shots yet, simply work following inside and getting the chin hook.

Round 2

Repeat the above, but once you follow inside, apply two quick body hooks post chin hook then wheel out of the clinch.

Round 3

Repeat the getting inside aspect of round one, but here fire two uppercuts to the body then wheel out.

Round 4

Free form. Work getting inside and to the chin hook clinch. Once there, free form your hammering to the body, wheel out and repeat.

In a pinch solo training

Although not a perfect correlate, I find the following useful for when you simply want to work this tactic and partners happen to be scarce.

● Tie a standard bedsheet or bath towel around your heavy bag at shoulder height.
● Bang from the outside as prescribed in round one, then move

in for a head-drive clinch and slide off to your ear.
● Hook your chin over the tied sheet.
● You will not be able to apply much downward pressure, but the sheet can act as enough of a tactical mnemonic to work the preceding drills.

Keep in mind, the chin hook clinch is not for the long haul. That is, extended sessions inside the clinch. But for quick weighting of your opponent and rapid shots to the body it has more than enough to recommend it.

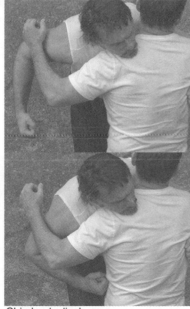

Chin hook clinch.

20. Tommy Farr & pit fighting

In 1986, John Hackleman launched his gym, The Pit, thus fighters from this base were known as pit fighters. The most renowned of these pit fighters was former UFC light heavyweight champion Chuck Liddell.

Pit fighting was in actuality a harder form of Hawaiian kempo, which in itself was formerly known as kajukenbo, yet another hybrid martial art originating in Hawaii in the

From collection of Brian Jenkins

late 1940s. The admittedly awkward word, kajukenbo, was meant to do honor to the arts that constituted its whole: karate, judo, jujitsu, kenpo and boxing. Not a bad mix at all.

Kajukenbo still survives under that original name, with some branches calling itself Hawaiian kenpo. Coach Hackleman ballparking on Hawaiian kempo (note the "m") to emphasize the harder approach to training and application that he advocates.

I'm sure you noticed that so far the arts we have discussed are Eastern in origin. Exactly how do we get to our discussion to boxing? Back to the phrase "pit fighting." We simply needed to distinguish between what is known in modern parlance as pit fighting and the far, far more brutal game of pit fighting that entertained Welsh miners. Our best look at Welsh "ymladd pwll" (pit fighting from here on out) comes to us from the rugged boxer Tommy Farr. Farr, whose ring name confounds the ears, "The Tonypandy Terror," is best known for his controversial fight with heavyweight champion Joe Louis on March 15, 1937. Joe earned the 15-round decision, but there are those who see otherwise.

Back to why we're discussing Mr. Farr. Tommy was born on March 12, 1913 in Wales. (To be exact he was born in Clydach Vale, Rhondda — you gotta love Welsh spellings.) As many did in his time and locale, he started young as a coal miner. How young? He was twelve-years old. Tough occupation plus tough lads equals maturation to tough men. Tommy was no exception. He was underground during a not uncommon mine explosion and carried scars his entire life.

Now what exactly did Welsh colliers do for recreation during down time? Well, it seems they indulged in a bit of pit fighting—and we are not talking kajukenbo or Hawaiian kempo or kenpo. So what exactly is pit fighting, Welsh style? Two holes are dug waist deep approximately two feet apart. Contestants enter the holes, face off and commence battering one another. Unable to flee or effectively duck, the game is one of blocking and being the hardest hitting man willing to fling while waist deep in a hole. You win by so incapacitating the other fellow in his hole that he cannot fire back. Keep in mind being unable to fall when knocked out resulted in a bit more punishment than normal boxing. Ah, the grand ol' days of good clean fun.

Mr. Farr enjoyed a fine ring career and one cannot help but presume that pit fighting aided and abetted his upper body defensive game and bolstered the fighting spirit by the sheer grit of the endeavor.

Four rounds of "soft" pit fighting
Here are a few drill variations to shake up your game and grab a bit of Tommy Farr-ness without actually having to stand in a hole and take a shot to the mouth.

Shoe lace drill
Tie your shoelaces together and work the heavy bag, pads and (very) light sparring. Strive to stay stock still as you can.

Box drill
Stand inside an 18-inch by 18-inch square and work the heavy bag, pads and, again, light sparring.

Paper drill
Stand on two sheets of notebook paper, one foot on each sheet. Work heavy bag, pads and light sparring. Any lift of the foot from the paper will be read immediately.

One-handed Bowie drill
There is a legend that the notorious frontiersman, Jim Bowie, once conducted a knife duel where each participant held a knife in the lead hand and each held one end of a single length of rope or chain in the other.

Here we will substitute a boxing glove for the knife. You will have more mobility than in the previous drills, but this freedom is more than made up for by the push-me/pull-you aspect of the "tug-of-war."

Even if we cannot or do not desire to engage in a true pit fight, these drills can go a long way to shaking up our game and provide a taste of what standing-in-a-hole strictures were like.

Shoe lace drill.

Paper drill.

One-handed Bowie drill.

Box drill.

21. Johnny Wilson's body-killing & hand-saving tactics

Born Giovanni Panica, this early middleweight champion fought under the name Johnny Wilson. He picked up the title in 1920 with a decision over Mike O'Dowd. While not a heavy hitter he was a fine technician who preferred to let his

opponents fight for him. By that I mean he often drew his fighters, or encouraged them to come to him. He'd stymie the incoming gambit with a jab, hit a little wheel-out and then work the hook. As a southpaw he found he had great success with the cumulative damage of this tactic.

Here's Mr. Wilson himself on how he took the title from O'Dowd:

Library of Congress

"I had no trouble outpointing him because he became furious, like a bulldog. That I loved. All I had to do was wait for him to come in and just jab, counter, hook. As the fight went along I started weakening him with left hooks to the stomach. I was more of a body puncher. I never believed in hitting a man in the jaw because I thought it was a little bit too hard. You break your hands on them."

Wilson was working in an era of lighter gloves when hand injuries could be more likely. But if we already have fragile hands, or if we simply want to build on the wisdom of exploiting unmatched stances, there's a lot to be learned here.

Four rounds Johnny Wilson style

Since this is all counter work, it is ideally worked on the pads with a feeder entering so you have something to work with.

Round 1
● The feeder steps in.
● The boxer jabs, don't worry about power. Flick it fast.
● Then immediately wheel the rear foot to the outside.

Round 2
● Repeat the above drill, but here add throwing a rear hook to the body after the wheel. The body is wide open for it in this position. Recall that Wilson was a southpaw, so when he says "left hook" he's talking about his rear hand.

Round 3
● Despite Johnny's talk of saving the hands and banging the body, he used the exact same sequence but ended with a rear hook to the chin to put O'Dowd on the canvas once.
● With that in mind, let's drill round two again, but this time make that rear hook on the button.

Round 4
● Have your feeder rush and you work the flick jab to wheel-out to mixing up the levels on that rear hook until it feels nice and crisp.

Southpaws have a lot of experience working unmatched leads. Orthodox fighters far less so unless they take the time to work unmatched tactics BEFORE they need them.

Step, jab, pivot.

Rear hook body.

Lead hook head.

22. Two-fisted, body-killing Pete "Kid" Herman style

Pete Herman was and is considered one of the best bantamweights of all time. Nat Fleischer of the legendary *Ring* magazine ranked him in the #2 spot right behind George "Little Chocolate" Dixon.

> His style was more about the physical wear of a furious work rate and banging the body often with two-fisted abandon.

In a long career that spanned 1912-1922, he held the bantamweight championship twice, fought 145 bouts, won 61 of those with 20 KOs and only lost 13 times. (Those extra bouts in that 145 tally can be chalked up to being the days of no-decision bouts.)

His KO numbers may appear low, but that is likely due to his preference to working inside and killing the body. His style was more about the physical wear of a furious work rate and banging the body often with two-fisted abandon. His incessant, unflagging pace was attributed to his training methods. He was yet another adherent of the "lumberjack method" of conditioning. He said, "I used to chop wood, saw logs, chop trees down, run early in the morning on the road. I used to rough it."

But what about that two-fisted, body-killing style? There's many a good body puncher in the game, but often these are set-up men, that is, those who probe the head and then land a good bang or two to the body. Kid Herman on the other hand was a real get-in-there-and-dig fighter. Many a boxing journalist said his style was developed in his youth in New Orleans where he grew up as a bootblack, aka shoeshine boy.

This sounds like a bit of Mr. Miyagi "wax on, wax off" mythmaking to me. If simply shining shoes made good fighters, I'd say we'd hear more about old-timers and wise fighters of today picking up a can of Kiwi shoe polish and getting to work. They didn't. They went to the gym and so did Mr. Herman.

He purposefully built his own in-fighting style and that had little to do with mirror sheens in shoes. He said, "I wasn't considered a terrific puncher. My best was at infighting. I used to use both hands to the body and that won a lot of fights for me, close quarters." Mr. Herman knew where his strength lay. Not necessarily in strong single shots, but getting inside, head on the chest or on the shoulder or in the face and banging away.

With that body-killing wisdom in mind, let's get to work Pete Herman style.

Fourteen rounds of two-fisted, body-killing combinations Kid Herman style

Put in at least a solid round of each and, as you might have guessed, all of these are to the body. Play it live. Get inside at the start of each combo and swing like you mean it.

- Jab/ cross
- Lead hook/ rear hook
- Cross/ lead hook
- Lead uppercut /rear uppercut
- Lead uppercut/ rear hook
- Rear uppercut/ lead hook
- Lead hook/ lead uppercut
- Double lead hook
- Double rear hook
- Cross/ lead hook/ cross
- Lead hook/ rear hook/ lead uppercut/ rear uppercut
- Lead uppercut/ rear uppercut/ lead hook/ rear hook
- Lead hook/ rear uppercut/ lead uppercut/ rear hook
- Lead uppercut/ rear hook/ lead hook/ rear uppercut/ lead hook

Whether it came from days as a bootblack or hours in the gym, no one can deny that a little body-killin' will turn many a tide for the in-fighter. It worked for one of the best, so why not us?

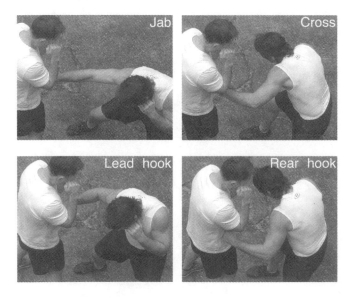

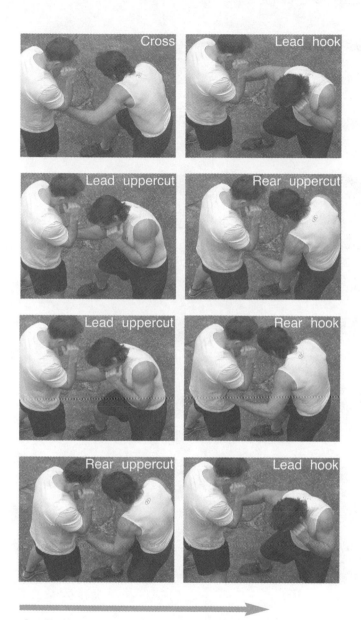

Combinations on pages 110-113 read left to right.

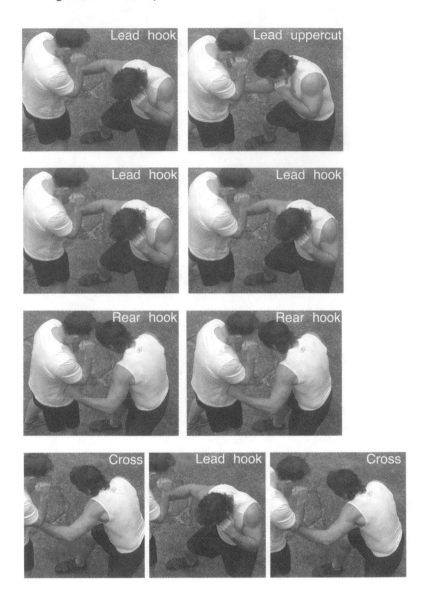

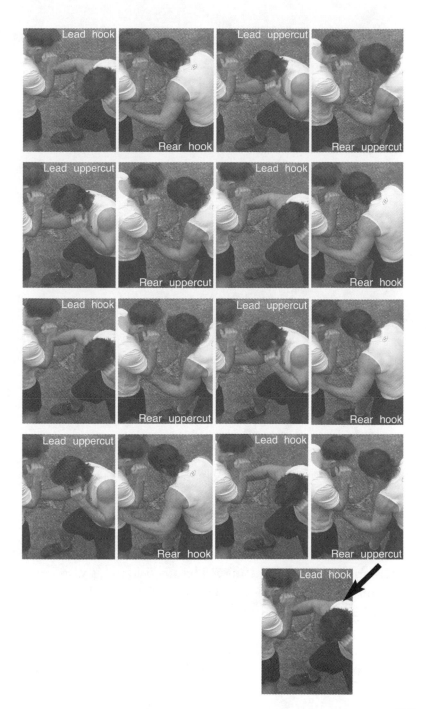

113

23. Tommy Burns' darting lead hook

Who doesn't love an underdog?

Tommy Burns was such an underdog and it's seldom remembered today, which is a bit of a mystery. Consider this: Tommy "The Little Giant of Hanover" Burns was a heavyweight champion of the world. Seems like that should

count for something, doesn't it? He was the first "World" champion to truly take that globe thing seriously. He travelled internationally to defend his title. Not a thing done at the time. Also, he took on all comers. He didn't hide behind a race line. He said he would fight anyone. This was an unfortunate rarity in the early days of the game.

This is Mr. Burns' view of things. "I will defend my title against all comers, none barred. By this I mean white, black, Mexican, Indian, or any other nationality. I propose to be the champion of the world, not the white, or the Canadian, or the American. If I am not the best man in the heavyweight division, I don't want the title." He was true to his word and fought all comers. He ties Larry Holmes for consecutive title defenses by stoppage (eight of 'em.)

And yet this champion is not highly regarded and seemingly barely remembered. If he is brought up it is because of his loss of the title to the then pariah, Jack Johnson. But consider this: Tommy Burns stepped up to face Johnson when most did not have the guts to do so. He was true to his all-comers creed. He was man-handled in that fight, but he comported himself like a champion.

Also, keep this in mind. Burns stood five foot, seven inches, the shortest champ in history. And he was light. I'm talking very light. At the time of his loss to Johnson, the challenger was at least six foot and weighed more than 200 pounds. The champion, Tommy Burns, came in at 168 1/2 pounds. WTF! At the very least a 30-pound weight disadvantage? Hmm? A much shorter, much smaller man lost to a larger, stronger, very capable fighter. Where's the shame in that?

So keep Burn's height and size in context when we examine his championship reign. It's not so much that he wasn't there all that long as it was that he was there at all. He was a "heavyweight" in name only yet performing so well against men much larger than himself.

There is something to be learned there. First, what is not to be learned—those low hands. Tommy was fast and, as we saw in Roy Jones Jr.'s younger days, able to get away with keeping his hands low. This is a fast, young fighters' gambit. If you've got the speed and the talent it can and has worked for some, but it seldom works for most of us. And even less seldom does it work for these very fighters as they age and mother nature takes a little speed out of that step. Start with good habits and they will see you through a longer career (think Bernard Hopkins).

What can we learn? That fast in-out style, particularly that darting lead hook.

Building Burns' darting lead hook

Unlike the champ, we will keep our hands high throughout.

Round 1
● Get in front of the mirror and work on the in-out footwork.
● Throw zero punches, just think in-out, fast and watch for over extending your balance.
● If at the end of the round any in-and-out felt off (you'll know it) repeat until you can gain confidence in your balance.

Round 2
● Let's take it to the bag, but rather than Burn's lead hook let's use the jab because the straight-line punching will allow us to better maintain the in-and-out dart while we learn to fire at the same time.

Round 3
● Once we have mastered the mechanics of Round 2, let's turn that in-out jab into a lead hook.
● Get on the bag and find that sweet spot where your lead hook is landing at the exact moment of your dart in.
● Immediately get out and monitor for any over-extension or out-of-balance moments.

Working in and out without punching.   Working in and out with jab.

Working in and out with hook.

Stepping inside a hook with a hook and stepping out.

Round 4
● Now, here's where we can utilize the full intent of Burn's darting hook. He used it as an inside hook. He would read an incoming shot, get inside the power curve to take some stink off of it and get that hook home and then be gone.
● Get with a good pad feeder and have them give you a big outside lead swing for you to read as you work darting in and out with that hook.

Round 5
● Still with your feeder, have them serve up a big rear swing that you can read.
● Read it, dart in, plant that hook and get out.

Round 6
● Still on the pads, this time allow your feeder to mix up the lead and rear swings so you learn the subtleties of that inside hook versus the two angles.

Repeat the preceding steps as many times as necessary looking for speed, power and timing.

Current rules don't allow for such mismatches as Burns faced when taking on Johnson. So if we keep our hands high and play Tommy's game right our darting lead hook may pay us better returns than this underrated champ got from it.

24. Panama Brown's up fist

This is one of those no longer strictly kosher tactics that may not fly today with a close observation from the referee, but it is still a fascinating excursion into historical uses for the scholar, the MMA striker and the sneak tactician.

Panama Al Brown, aka "The Elongated Panamanian" was from, take a guess? Mr. Brown held the bantamweight championship from 1929 till 1935. He was, as his ring name suggests, a tall lanky fighter with a surprising reach for his weight class (76 inches). He also carried quite a wallop for such a rangy fighter. It is likely this combination of reach and power that kept him on top for so long.

But what can't be ruled out was his occasional use of unorthodox angles. Mr. Brown found ways to make that reach work for him on the negative aspects of the punch. In other words, he meant his punch, but he also meant his retractions. Let's delve into just one aspect of this interesting tactic.

The right way to throw a jab body is from bent knees in order to throw a level punch with shoulder protection.

A downhill punch leaves the head exposed. Not recommended, but Panama made it work for him.

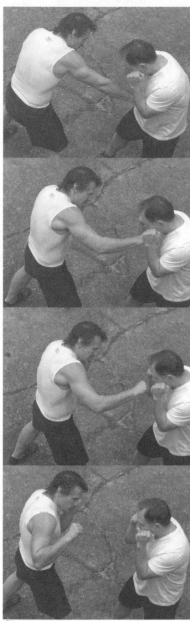

Panama Brown's up fist

Round 1

● Let's start on the heavy bag and actually engage in a boxing no-no.

● Brown could and did get away with "punching downhill." That is, he could, say, throw a long jab to the body without the usually wise corresponding dip in the knees so that he gets his shoulder behind the punch and not leave his jaw exposed.

● Brown likely got away with it often enough because of his reach and power. We'll get to that in a minute.

● First, for this round work the bag with long jabs to the body. Punch downhill while doing so. Don't exaggerate it, just break the usual good form for a round or so.

Round 2

● Now take this downhill jab to the mirror.

● On the retraction allow the hand to travel in an upward arc back to good defensive position.

● Start this arc at the end of the punch where the impact would be.

Showing the upward arc of the retracted jab.

Another angle of the retracted, downhill jab. The up fist makes contact with the opponent's chin.

Round 3
- Let's go back to the bag and punch downhill, but this time we will retract on the arc we worked in the mirror.
- It won't feel like anything…yet.

Round 4
- This round is best worked with a pad feeder who is also wearing a belly pad for body punching.
- Here, bang that downhill jab, retract as we have practiced with your feeder placing a pad in an uppercut feed.
- Allow the back of the jabbing fist to strike this pad on the way back.
- Don't exaggerate this movement, allow it to become part and parcel of the downhill jab retraction.
- It's best if you mean the jab and don't focus on the retraction, allow it to occur naturally.

Mr. Brown's tactic works best versus an opponent who vacuums or sucks in versus that body shot. If he doesn't vacuum your retraction will bite air, but if you meant the jab in the first place you still sought your mark. If the up-fist retraction bites on the way home, well, we can thank Panama Al Brown for this addition to our bag of tricks.

25. Luther McCarthy's "Betsy"

Due to his untimely death few recall the man that was Luther McCarthy. Let's rectify that. First, his name. 21st-century sources list his name as Luther McCarty with no "h"

following the letter "t." Every single one of my resources from 1911 to 1931 have the spelling as McCarthy. These sources being closer to the time this fine boxer walked the planet, I'll stick with them.

Born in Hitchcock County, Nebraska March 20th, 1892, he was called "Luck" by his family. Raised on a ranch he came up in the cowboy lifestyle and could ride and rope well. During his brief career he would appear on the vaudeville stage and regale the audience with his lariat abilities. His Nebraska origins and cowboy skills led to the ring names of "The Cowboy" or "The Fighting Cowboy." McCarthy was a big powerful man, well over six feet tall, some sources have him four inches taller. He possessed an 80-inch reach and used that to great effect whipping jabs with equal facility to an opponent's body and face.

McCarthy was active during the unfortunate days of rampant and vicious racism. In particular to our story, the days of the almost feral hunt for a "Great White Hope" to dethrone the dominant and perceived pariah, Jack Johnson.

McCarthy was a natural contender for this "Hope Hunt." On New Year's Day 1913, McCarthy fought Al Palzer for the despicably named World White Heavyweight Champion. McCarthy picked up the manufactured title and defended it successfully against challenger "Fireman Flynn" in April of that year. Two weeks later (two weeks!) he beat the very tough Frank Moran (also covered in these pages.)

On May 24th, 1913, he takes a "stay busy" fight with a Canadian boxer by name of Arthur Pelkey. No one considered Pelkey a dangerous challenge to McCarthy. In the first round after what appeared to be a light punch to the heart, McCarthy drops to the canvas. He was pronounced dead shortly thereafter. A coroner's jury absolved Pelkey and boxing of the death and attributed it to a bad tumble from a horse a few weeks before the fight and surmised that the shot to the heart triggered an underlying injury from that fall.

There is a particularly poignant photo taken of McCarthy on the canvas with light streaming from above. I do not include it as we are here to celebrate McCarthy's life and accomplishments and not lay mildly curious eyes on his lifeless form.

McCarthy was known for his power, his calm demeanor in the ring, his good use of that long jab, a dynamite left hook to the body and…"Betsy." What was Betsy? Betsy was his long whipping rear uppercut. Mighty fine fighter Carl Morris had never been on the canvas before his bout with McCarthy. Journalist George Lemmer reports that Betsy lifted Morris off his feet before dumping him to unfamiliar canvas territory.

Most of his KOs or major damage was the result of this unusual uppercut. So was Betsy simply a good strong uppercut thrown by a powerful man? Yes, but also a bit more than that.

Six rounds to throwing Betsy

Round 1
● Get in front of your mirror and envision an opponent in your usual rear uppercut range.
● Now, take one slide-step rearward out of your usual comfortable range.
● Throw your uppercut from this extended position; the angle of your forearm and upper arm will have to open up to allow you to strike at this distance.
● Watch the mirror as the punch swings down and then up.

Round 2
● Turn your profile to the mirror so you can get a better handle on how soon to begin this opening loop or swing.

Round 3
● Take Betsy to the heavy bag or pads.
● Throw a few feelers with your standard rear uppercut, then take that sliding step back.
● The bag will really reveal where and when you need to open up that elbow angle.
● You'll want to concentrate on turning the rear hip just a bit rearward, then as the hip uncoils whip that rear arm down throwing in an almost upward arcing swing rather than a proper uppercut.
● Just before impact use an aggressive snap from your biceps and front deltoid to whip this swing into the target.

Round 4
● Put your head on the bag and bang a standard inside rear uppercut.
● Then slide step back and slam a Betsy.
● Slide back into the inside position and work these two in an alternating manner.

Throwing a rear uppercut normal range.

Stepping back and throwing an extended rear uppercut or Betsy.

Round 5
● Let's put Betsy into combination and use one of McCarthy's own.
● Jab/ rear straight/ lead hook/ Betsy
● Your aim is to fire them all from a just outside position.

Round 6
● One more McCarthy combination to make Betsy feel at home.
● Lead with a rear straight follow it with a lead hook and add Betsy as the vicious cherry on top.

Fate and circumstances being what they are, we will never know how McCarthy might have fared against Johnson or any other fighter for that matter. But we do know that many of the skills and accomplishments of his short life are well worth study by students of martial endeavor.

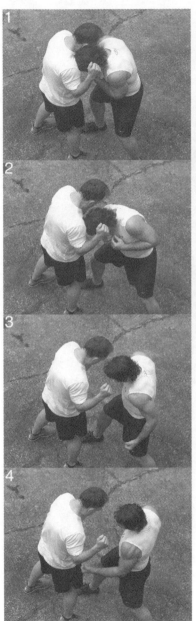

Stepping back from a clinch after throwing a lead uppercut and delivering a Betsy.

Firing from a step outside—jab, rear straight and Besty combo.

26. Parsing Marciano's trailing forearm

There is a famous photo of Marciano slamming a big left hook into the crafty Jersey Joe Walcott. If we look closely at that photo, we see that after the punch has landed that lead forearm trails right behind and adds to the wallop. You can find instances of this trailing forearm all over The Rock's fights. Again, his "use" of the tactic was likely accidental or incidental, part and parcel of a 100 percent slamming style. But let's say if you wanted to throw such a trailing forearm purposefully, how would one go about doing it?

In the early days of boxing, the bootleg days, the boombattle days, the days when some fighters had more than a few extra tools at their disposal or there were no regulating bodies to decide what's kosher, such a forearm would be called a "hacksaw." (See our book, *No Holds Barred Fighting: Savage Strikes* for the lowdown on such illegal blows.) By strict definition, a hacksaw would be an intended forearm, whereas a trailing forearm was just "dems the breaks" in boxing.

Round 1
● Get in front of the mirror and throw your standard lead hook.
● With standard proper form we allow the fist to do all the work.
● That's good form and good sportsmanship.

Standard lead hook.

Round 2
● Now take it to the bag and repeat proper hooking.
● Make no attempt to trail at this time.
● Let's just pay very close attention to how we throw it correctly.

Round 3
● This time, let's get on the bag and stand, say, 10-12 inches outside of our standard hook range.
● Let's take a lunging step to get that hook to the target. Again, make no attempt to trail just yet, simply execute the lunging hook.

Round 4
● This time set up for the lunging hook, but aim at the bag for the fist to just skim the surface of the bag. If you have a good bag swivel you'll likely set the bag to spinning with each hook.

Round 5
● Let's repeat that lunging/skimming hook on the bag. But allow your forward lunge to carry you (awkwardly) to the bag so that your skimming fist rolls off and your trailing forearm rakes the radius and sometimes a bit of elbow over the bag.

Again, the Rock never seems to be skimming his hooks, he means them all and the trailing forearm is part of his lunging style. But by learning to skim on the heavy bag, then on the pads (or an opponent if you are a little less than reputable in character), you mean both the hook (no skim) and the trailing forearm. Again, for entertainment purposes only, but that's how it was done.

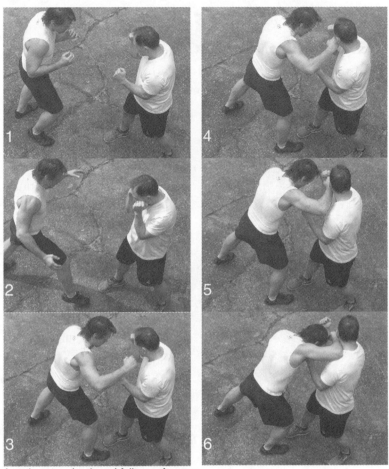

Lunging step, hook and followup forearm.

27. Ken Norton's personal one-two

One of the things that come to mind when one thinks of the beast that was Ken Norton—that physique. It is easy to overlook these days when thanks to easy access to pharmaceuticals even non-athletes can look like athletes. Ken Norton looked like he could have easily made the casting call for the film *300*. His was not show muscle. It was bona fide, hard-earned, hard-won power.

> Just how canny and formidable? Lest one forget, Mr. Norton handed Ali his second career defeat, breaking his jaw in the doing.

And his skill inside the ring was not based solely on this power. He had skills. He could punch in bunches, put combinations together that baffled, and the fact that each of those baffling fists had that much stink on them made them all the more formidable. Just how canny and formidable? Lest one forget, Mr. Norton handed Ali his second career defeat, breaking his jaw in the doing.

Mr. Norton may have held the heavyweight title for only a brief time, but his years in and around the top were never mistaken for an also ran. He was always fearsome, ring-ready and nobody's chump. We've mentioned his power and his ready ability to punch in combination, let's take just one of those combos, a mere two-pointer, and put it together Ken Norton style.

As far as the physique and power goes, well, we'll have to suffer with what we've got.

Root one-two: Lead hook to the body/ rear uppercut to jaw

Mr. Norton had a pressing, almost "walk 'em down" style. He used his power and conditioning to keep the pressure on. It was usually within the context of this press that he would fire his best combinations. Often his go-tos were based on sound boxing strategy—kill the body and the head will follow. You want a clean shot to the head? Bring the hands down. How? Bang the body.

We'll take a single Ken Norton favorite and apply it in a variety of ways just as he did so effectively.

Round 1
● Step in and fire both.

Lead hook body, rear uppercut head.

Round 2
● Fire the lead hook from the outside then slide in for the rear uppercut.

Round 3
● Fire the lead hook from the outside then slide in to put your head on the bag or partner, then fire the rear uppercut.

Round 4
● Start with your head on the bag or on a partner, give a slight shoulder bump to open up the lead hook and throw the rear uppercut right behind it.

Round 5
● Start with your head on the bag or a partner, fire the lead hook, slide step out and bang the rear uppercut.

Mr. Norton was more than just his physique. He had swift hands, good angles and, oh yes indeed, he put that powerful physique to work for him. If we are wise, we'll all become as strong as we can support with our frame without sacrificing speed. But in the meantime, let's work craftiness Ken Norton style from day one.

See images for combo variations pages 137-141.

Stepping in with a lead hook, rear uppercut and stepping out.

Outside lead hook, sliding in with rear uppercut and stepping out.

Outside lead hook, sliding in, putting head on opponent and firing rear uppercut.

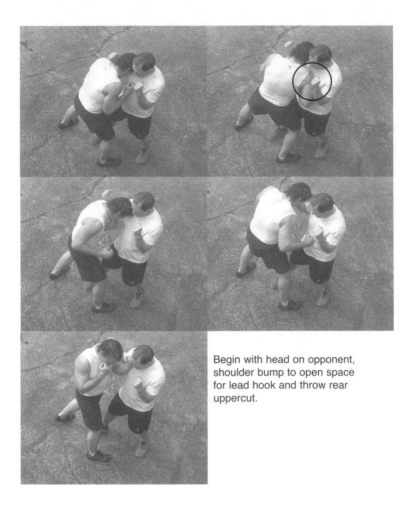

Begin with head on opponent, shoulder bump to open space for lead hook and throw rear uppercut.

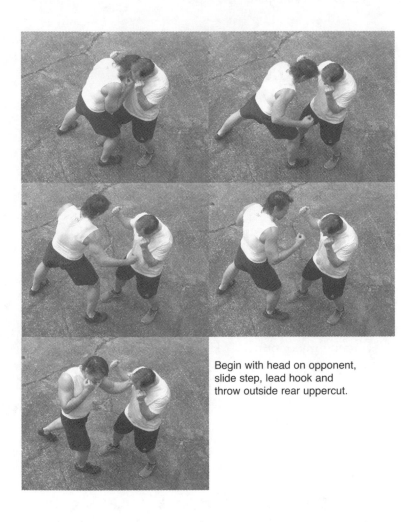

Begin with head on opponent,
slide step, lead hook and
throw outside rear uppercut.

28. Salvador Sanchez's "short hook"

I can say with all certitude that if Salvador Sanchez's life wasn't cut short in an auto accident his name would be better known. He was only 23 years old when he died, but in that short career he racked up 44 wins with only one loss and one draw. He also picked up a featherweight crown along the way.

Fans of crafty fighters such as Sugar Ray Leonard, Jose Napoles and Ruben Olivares will find much to admire here. You'll also see those fighters reflected in Sanchez's style because the three fighters were his own heroes. He was never a big puncher and relied on his craftiness and artistry to do the work. As he put it, "The KOs come through undermining my opponent." He had something right, because although not heavy handed he still racked up 32 knockouts.

We will take just one of Sanchez's many crafty tools and pick it apart for our own use and allow this to guide us when we examine everything else in our own arsenals.

Salvador Sanchez's "short hook"
Mr. Sanchez could feint with the best of them, but where many use feints in stuttered, half measures, Sanchez would often throw full-blown punches to get the reaction he desired. We'll drill one to see what he was up to.

Round 1
● Get on the bags or pads and throw a lead hook to a rear straight combination.
● Make no attempt to feint, just do the job

Round 2
● This time feint the lead hook as is standardly done, then throw that rear straight with some stink on it.

Round 3
● This is where we feint Salvador Sanchez style. Just outside of range throw that lead hook —I mean throw it—but miss with it. In other words, do not commit to the distance for it to actually land. Stay just outside of range.
● Get used to throwing and missing without losing balance.

Round 4
● Throw that short Sanchez hook and slide right behind it with a rear straight with all the bad intentions you can muster.

Sanchez would often not open himself with trying to get inside to the bang. He would allow these "real" punches thrown short to prompt reactions and also to protect him as he was out of range himself. When the prompted reaction was given, such as a float of a hand to protect the hook, the other hand was fired home. If we are wise, we will use some of Mr. Sanchez's undermining wisdom

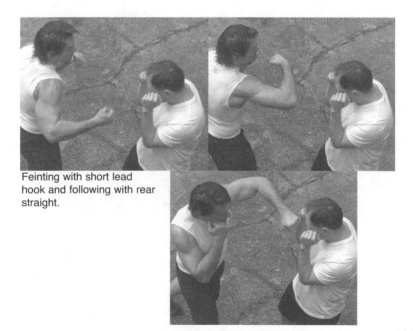

Feinting with short lead hook and following with rear straight.

1. Master trainer on training for toughness

You'll have to tolerate a paragraph or two from me before we get to the meat of this lesson—some wise words from a master trainer on training for toughness. Who is the master trainer I speak of? Jimmy DeForest. For those not in the know, Jimmy DeForest was the boxing trainer and conditioning coach for these luminaries:

Jack Dempsey
Stanley Ketchel
James J. Jeffries
Joe Gans
George Dixon
Joe Walcott
Kid McCoy
Tommy Ryan
Philadelphia Pal Moore
Jack Sharkey
Luis Angel Firpo

That is quite a stable of leather-tough, nail-spittin', hard-hittin' hombres if there ever was one. These men all share in common heavy hands, no quit in the tank and to-the-marrow toughness. So what was it that DeForest thought was so important?

Toughness. Robustness.

What is robustness? It is not merely the conditioning one does (which is all-fire important]), it is also the circumstances, the environment, the overall "feel" or vibe that training is conducted in. It is un-smoothing the gym; it is un-boxing the athlete; it is getting rid of any and all comfort while the uncomfortable work is being done.

Let's turn the floor over to Mr. DeForest:

New York World Syndicate

"[In the early days] the fighters came to the ring properly conditioned to do their best for the particular distance they were required to go—six, eight, ten, or fifteen rounds. For the most part they were fighters toughened by far more rigorous training methods than are employed today, and able to battle hard for fifteen rounds and be fresh at the finish.

"There were no 'hot-house' fighters a generation ago. The men didn't have the money for expensive camps and imported chefs. They trained in cold barns, and when they wanted a shower, they stood under a big can in which holes had been punched while someone poured in a bucket of cold water from above. Rigorous treatment, but it made tough bodies. Men would go fifteen, twenty, and twenty-five rounds and show scarcely a mark afterwards. Nowadays blood flows freely in almost every six round go."

Mr. DeForest penned those words in 1930. This before the age of air conditioning (or air cooling as it was termed then), efficient heating or anything that we encounter in even the marginally equipped commercial gym of today. Imagine how much more shade he would throw at today's training environments. Imagine the look in the eyes from that stable of fighters as they view our comfy "boxes" from the vantage point of their bare bones proving grounds. Probably the same look a hungry coyote has when it sees the pampered pet let out onto the manicured lawn to relieve itself and get back inside where it's all nice and cozy.

To capture a bit of the old school toughness and fearsome fighting ability, perhaps it's more than merely duplicating tactics and going through the motions of similar conditioning. Perhaps there is as much to be said for duplicating the environment as well. If a man as knowledgeable as Mr. DeForest thought so, who are we to say he's wrong?

A few suggestions on toughening up the training environment

● Get outside with any and all training that is conducive. Roadwork, rope skipping, hell, even pad work. Year-round, hot or cold, rain or shine.

● When indoors, turn off that thermostat if you have the opportunity. Work in the hot or cold environment that the day's weather offers you.

● End the post-training shower with a 30-second burst of cold water. Learn to tolerate that end-of-relaxing-shower unpleasantness.

● If you incorporate resistance training in your program, skip machines and opt for free weights.

● Or go the prior suggestion one better and opt for resistance training with unusual objects. Throw tires, lift stones, lift and toss logs.

The above are just a few ideas to get the flavor of Mr. DeForest's insight. One can never tell what will provide the edge between good and great, bad and badder, between small "t" tough and capital "T" TOUGH.

2. Kid McCoy's "shoelace trick"

We discussed the mighty colorful Charles "Kid" McCoy in the first volume of our dip into past mastery. Colorful is a weak word to describe the life of this man full of deeds both famous and infamous. He was a celebrated hard

puncher, making *The Ring Magazine's* list of "The 100 Greatest Punchers of All Time" at 74, That may be deep in the rankings, but that still puts him ahead of Roy Jones, Jr., Evander Holyfield and The Pampas Bull himself, Luis Firpo. He was also thought of so highly that in the 1958 volume *Fifty Years at Ringside* he was ranked the #1 Light Heavyweight of All Time.

What we want to point to in this lesson has zero to do with punching power and everything with McCoy's gift for bending the truth. Let's look to an episode where that truth bending didn't occur outside the ring with the press, but a bit of out-and-out fakery inside the ring that led to a wholly on-the-level KO.

McCoy, never one to shy away from seeming mismatches, accepted a fight with a giant of a fighter named Plaascke who is reported to have outweighed McCoy by 100 pounds. Reports at ringside have it that McCoy actually used the following tactic: He pointed to Plaascke's shoes and said, "Your shoe is untied." Plaascke glanced down and McCoy being McCoy unleashed some of that vaunted power and walked off with the victory.

Now, this may not be a directly transferable lesson. Few may respond to a shoelace trick, but some may. What we can do, if we are fighters who have a penchant for such showmanship-based tactics, is to use a variety of head games to discombobulate.

I offer the following short list of possible tactics in the vein of McCoy's shoelace trick.

● Look off—A sudden look to the side as if something has caught your attention.
● Sound off—A verbal response or "reply" to a pretended query from a corner.
● Shoes untied—Frequent looks towards the opponent's shoes as if to say so with the eyes.
● False stop—A sudden drop of hands (out of range, of course) and false turn back to the corner as if the round were over
● Sniff test—Quick sniff of your own glove followed by an expression as if to say "What's that?"

In short, any seemingly mundane behavior that elicits a response that leads to an opening. And who knows, maybe, just maybe if you have the chutzpah or cojones make a stab at the McCoy original and see if it still has legs.

3. Charley Goldman & Angelo Dundee: "Be you, but more so"

Charley Goldman was a legendary trainer and true to his name he struck gold in one of his proteges, the also legendary Rocky Marciano. This lesson isn't about The Rock, per se, but there is more than a little bit of Marciano's key to success here. The equally

Library of Congress

Charley Goldman (right) with Al McCoy.

legendary trainer, Angelo Dundee, spent an apprenticeship with Charley Goldman and attributes much of his wisdom to things he learned while under his tutelage. One of those bits of strategic wisdom was what we shall call "Be you, but more so."

What do I mean by that? Goldman would evaluate his fighters and come up with strategies and tactics that fit their attributes. One of his keys was to put a finger on what you were, usually some obvious aspect, and then exaggerate that aspect. Here's Angelo Dundee in his own words on what Charley told him: "The thing I learned from Charley was, 'If they're short, make 'em shorter. If they're tall, make 'em taller.' So there's a tremendous amount of advice." Hence: "Be you, but more so."

How Goldman sought to implement this advice was to take his short fighters and make them hard to hit bundles of from-the-floor power. If the fighter was tall, he'd see to it that that reach, that body length, those long legs were exploited to their utmost. Goldman and Dundee recognized that many young fighters have an idol or two dancing and shadowboxing in their heads and sometimes the idol chosen does not necessarily match the actual physical characteristics of the worshipping fighter.

Look at it this way: Tommy "The Hitman" Hearns was an absolutely excellent fighter. You may love him to death, but if you stand 5 foot seven (Roberto Duran's height) no matter how close you can mimic The Hitman's moves you would still be a half a foot off from Hearns' six-one. And part of what made Tommy Tommy was his tall frame.

We are all wise to look to Mr. Goldman's eye on the realities of what the individual really is and go from there. Don't consider our shortness or tallness or whatever we are as detriments, but attributes to be exploited.

Or to repeat the five words: "Be you, but more so."

"Who are you?" assessment battery

Are you a tall or a short fighter?

Do you have long reach or average?

Are you physically strong or closer to average?

Are you quick or a bit closer to the mean in speed?

Are you fleet of foot or more methodical in footwork?

Are you a "burst" fighter or more of one that shows well over the long haul?

Are you an in-fighter or an out-fighter?

Do you excel at toe-to-toe or does the counter-fighting game fit your bill?

● Do you like showy tactics or is playing it close to the bone more your speed?

These are basic questions that I wager you can answer easily. Now, we all want to improve and be well rounded, and we should strive for that. To embody the advice is to improve all around, but put a very special eye and a good deal of attention on what is already pretty damn good or special about you and make it golden, Charley Goldman style.

4. Joe Louis and "working softly"

President Teddy Roosevelt once included in a speech the phrase "Speak softly and carry a big stick." Over time some have mis-remembered the phrase as "Walk softly and carry a big stick." It is that mis-remembered version of the phrase that aptly describes a tactic that trainer Mannie Seamon used when preparing Joe Louis for his return bout with Billy Conn.

Lest we forget, the faster and lighter Billy Conn, in their first bout, outmaneuvered The Brown Bomber and beat him to the punch more often than not until the 13th round when Conn got a bit greedy. Until that point, Conn was ahead on all scorecards and well on his way to a big upset of a bondafide ring legend. Then he decided he was good enough to trade power for power. He wasn't.

The rematch was looked to avidly by fans as it was figured that this time the speedier Conn would retain his speed and keep his greed in check and forgo trading power with the more powerful Brown Bomber. It was assumed that Joe Louis, powerful as he was, was not up to Conn's speed-

151

demon game and if things went that way he would lag behind. This is where Mannie Seamon landed on an idea that he used in the Billy Conn rematch and throughout Louis' later career. He had Joe's sparring ring covered by a ring canvas that overlay a surface that was 3/4-inch thicker than normal ring flooring. In *Corner Men* Ronald K. Fried writes, "His theory was that if Louis trained on a thick — and therefore slow—canvas, he would be much speedier on fight night when stepping on thinner canvas."

The rematch was practically Joe all the way with another knockout, this time in the 8th round. Whether it was the slow canvas training or Conn's erosion of skill after his stint in the service, who can say? But there does seem to be a bit of wisdom in "working softly" and "slowly" to gain speed on a standard competitive surface.

A few ideas to work soft & slow Joe Louis style
Doubled-ring surface
If we have the option to thicken our training surface as Mannie Seamon did for Joe, by all means give it a shot. I work on a double-thickness wrestling mat.

Varied surface
Failing that, one can also look to trying some unusual surface sparring sessions, or at least hard pad work days on eccentric surfaces. Try working on sand, grass or even marshy, muddy ground like a few bare knucklers did in the grand ol' days.

Viking rounds
One might even consider giving a go to an idea found in the Viking sagas where combatants would spar/fight/compete while standing in knee- or waist-deep water. Having tried it more than a few times myself, I can vouch for the fact that it plays hell with your movement, but after spending a good 1/2 hour immersed in water, once you get back to dry land you feel like you are moving whippet fast.

Double socks

There are some reports of old school fighters garnering the same results by training in two pairs of extra thick socks and/or extra-cushioned soles in their shoes so that when it comes fight night and time to don the regulation garb one feels fleet of foot. This method strikes me as a bit too little, but who knows?

No matter which tactic strikes your fancy, it is well worth it to give soft slow surfaces a try now and then for both the Joe Louis effect and to spice up a training session where some days feel that they need a little something new to shake it up.

> "...you notice... fighters...you stop while [they are] boxing, you pick up little pointers and these things you try, and this is what...makes a fighter improve."
>
> —Jack Sharkey

5. Jack Sharkey & the art of paying attention

Jack Sharkey was born Jouzas Zukauskas, the son of Lithuanian immigrants. It was in the Navy where he took up boxing and soon proved himself to be the terror of the fleet. After the Navy years he decided to turn pro and along the way shed himself of the name that was tough for many mouths to get around. He settled on Jack Sharkey which was a combination of two of his favorite boxers — Tom Sharkey and Jack Dempsey. There is something a wee bit significant in Sharkey choosing a name that combined styles. Sharkey was no mere slugger. He was a fighter with a brain, a man who considered studying styles and observing other fighters as part and parcel of the game.

How good was he? Well, if we consider just one bout, that against one of his idols, Jack Dempsey, we have a mighty big tell. On July 21st, 1927 the two were pitted against one another to determine who was going to have a go at newly crowned champ, Gene Tunney. So how did he do? For six rounds Sharkey outpointed one of his heroes handily and appeared to be on the track to overshadowing the better known Dempsey. In the 7th round, Sharkey turned to the referee to complain of a low blow, Dempsey caught him flush with a left hook during this head turn and that was all she wrote. (You can view the fight yourself. Was the punch low? Yep. A lotta low ones being flung there, surprised it wasn't called. Mr. Sharkey looked to me to being next to face Tunney.) So what was it that made this man good enough to make his idol look a bit awkward? The man was a student of the game. He paid attention. In a sense, his own two eyes were his coach and trainer. Let's let Mr. Sharkey speak:

"The reason you learn, it isn't too much from the trainers, it's from your own eyesight that you notice these fighters, standing around in the gym when you're waiting to go in to box or you're jumping rope or punching the bag, you stop while he's boxing, you pick up little pointers and these things you try, and this is what, if you've got any brains in your head at all, this is what makes a fighter improve. And you get so it's entirely different and easier than your own style, so this is how a smart fighter gets to be a great fighter. It's the fighter himself that can improve and try something."

Wise words, but how exactly might we put this into action?

Seeing through Jack Sharkey's eyes

● First things first, when in the gym, unplug. Leave the earbuds in the locker.
● Stow the phone.
● When not on the mat or in the ring watch. Look. See.
● Watch other fighters.
● Look at them all.
● Watch the best around you and pick out details that you think make them slick.
● Look at the newbies, or never-gonna-bes and diagnose what's going wrong.
● Don't allow any mistake or benefit to be invisible.
● If you can see it, if you can process it, you are at the first step to making a benefit your own or learning how to exploit common mistakes.

But if you ain't looking, you ain't never gonna see anything and you'll be left running your same groove. It will be your style, yes. But it will become a predictable style, something that someone else who is paying attention can exploit. Sharkey paid attention to Dempsey. Dempsey did not pay attention to Sharkey. A more attentive ref might have changed history.

> But if you ain't looking, you ain't never gonna see anything and you'll be left running your same groove.

Part 3

Training & Conditioning

1. Boxing & lumberjack connection

Many an early fighter came from the tough occupations that abounded in the early days. Mining camps, ranch work, keelboats and, of course, lumber camps.

> Jack Dempsey, Jack Johnson and Harry Greb...saw chopping wood as THE way to build ancillary power and wind for their boxing training.

These occupations were tough with a capital "T" and fostered strength and conditioning by dint of the very work itself. You take a job that requires grit, add to it that the very nature of the job increases strength and toughness, add the human animal's natural propensity for competition (I can chop faster than you!), add an occasional throwing of hands here and there and it's easy to see why so many fighters came from these occupational callings.

Many of these fighters took that calling with them when they entered the professional cadre and their ways of tough training became respected go-tos for fighters who themselves never saw the inside of a mining camp or lumberjack spread. Those fighters are too numerous to mention all, but you can count Jack Dempsey, Jack Johnson and Harry Greb among those who saw chopping wood as THE way to build ancillary power and wind for their boxing training. As we advanced through the modern age, chopping wood fell by the wayside for many as more modern methods began to hold sway. But more than a few powerful men still swore that there was no better way to build wind and power. The great George Foreman swore by wood chopping and no one doubted his power.

With that in mind, if we want to build power the old school way let's at least get it right. This offering is an old school PT challenge, a mini tutorial on form and a bit of a finger wag at an aspect of "functional" training. First the PT Challenge:

Lumberjack Tabata
Gear
● You
● An eastern single-bit ax (you can go double-bit, but you won't be shifting surfaces).
● A downed log to work (or if you've got a tree that needs to be felled, you've got a twofer — conditioning and chores).
● A timer set to Tabata intervals.

Protocol
● Hit that timer and chop furiously for 20 seconds.
● Rest for a strict 10 seconds.
● Then back on the stick for 20 more seconds.
● You do this for a total of 8 work rounds giving you a total of 2 minutes and 40 seconds of work.

For those unfamiliar with Tabata rounds and that seemingly paltry work ethic, if you're playing honestly the soul will cry as soon as you start your second 20-second interval. The 10-second "rest" will quickly reveal itself as woefully insufficient, BUT do not allow that to sandbag following rounds. Chop HARD, chop FAST.

For my history buffs, lumberjacks were noted in days of
yore (and days of now) as being mighty powerful creatures.
Many a boxer, wrestler and combination man (that won-
derful hybrid) used jack work as fight conditioners. It builds
strength, it builds stamina, it builds power and it teaches
more than a few things about mechanics. Many an old broad
swordsman augmented "playing at post" with the necessities
of "working the ax."

Don't be a rubber maid

In "functional" strength circles jack work has fallen out of
fashion and been replaced by smacking sledgehammers into
truck tires. A few unasked for thoughts on that faux badassery.
● Tires provide rebound, logs and rocks do not. Since when did
we want training wheels on our toughness?
● As for functional, when was the last time this scenario
occurred, "Come quick, there's been a storm and we need you
to beat the shit out of a tire!"

Let's allow my tire-smacking enthusiast to reply with "That's
an iffy argument, Mark. The mechanics of swinging a
hammer against the tire and chopping wood are similar and I
could easily transfer these skills, thus rendering my tire-
assaulting habit functional."

We will now pause as all who have ever actually felled wood,
hewn logs or worked a blade smile to ourselves and marvel
at the jejune assumptions.

A few rejoinders (just a few)

● True ax work will allow no rebound. You will work on both the
positive and the negative sides of the stroke, possibly more on
the negative which is the opposite of the tire experience. (We'll
come back to this.)
● True ax work requires precision. You must work furiously
while using eye-hand coordination to carve the kerf as needed.
Tire work is willy-nilly rebounding akin to Stanley Kubrick's

apish proto-humans at the beginning of *2001: A Space Odyssey.*
● True ax work requires alternating swings within the sprint set, often each stroke is alternating. That's how kerfs are carved. Most tire work is "swing from the right this round, switch to left that round. There, now you're cool!"

Mil.ru., creative commons

We could continue, but we see that this "functional" exercise is about as functional as beating up tires.

I'll allow General Georgi Zhukov to express the difference between theory and practice. He may be talking about large scale maneuvers, but the concept is the same.

"From the practice of the first operations I concluded that those commanders failed most often who did not visit the terrain where action was to take place themselves, only studied it on the map and issued written orders. The commanders who are to carry out combat missions [that's you, reader] must by all means know the terrain and enemy battle formations very well in order to take advantage of weak points in his dispositions and direct the main blows there."

Primer on how to swing an ax

Swing

● Square up to your log.
● Grip the subordinate hand at the grip (towards the end of the handle).
● Grip the dominant hand further up the handle towards the shoulder (the bit of handle near the ax head).
● Sight where you want to strike and swing HARD, sliding the dominant hand down the handle towards the grip as you make impact.
● That is the positive portion of the stroke.

Swing strategy

● Our next stroke should approach the first cut from the opposite side, so now you will have an angled cut from one side and then one from the other. You have started your kerf.
● Continue in that fashion alternating kerf sides slowly building your kerf away from the center—away from the initial cuts. This allows wood chips to fly out from the widening and deepening kerf clearing the way for each stroke.
● Building a kerf from the outside in, or worse, having no idea or plan on the chop will result in more than a few embarrassing "sticking the ax" moments.

Retrieval

● Every stroke into the wood should be treated as if the ax will stick.
● As soon as it makes impact, pump the rear hand upward on the ax handle hard while loosely gripping (or even letting go with the forward hand). This handle pump utilizes leverage to free the heel and blade from wood (or bone for my battle axe swingers).
● At the end of the pump arc, slide the forward hand back to the shoulder of the handle to lift the heavy ax head aloft. (You are using a heavy ax, right?)

All of the above is executed in smooth strokes at a furious pace. Power, stamina, eye-hand coordination, impact mechanics, a taste of battle axe revelry, functional skill, maybe a little wood for the fire or chores completed. So which one of these two activities is the functional one again? And if you are still thinking slinging the sledge is still kinda the same thing, well, it is if you are breaking rocks doing muck-work, not beating tires. (Another day, another beef with faux functional.)

Keep in mind, holding a big boy toy don't make you a big boy. (Entendre acknowledged and accurate.)

"Let not thy will roar, when thy power can but whisper."
—Thomas Fuller

*So to us all being strong man Jacks and Jills hewing wood like a highball outfit, earning our hayward lightning and having tighter sleeves and not be sweenied and have the sap to shove a nose down when we need to.

*Lumberjack glossary
Hayward Lighting — Homemade brew. Notoriously strong.
Highball Outfit — A hard working, knowledgeable crew.
Sap — Wherewithal.
Shove a Nose Down — Thrash an opponent easily.
Sweenied — Shrunken muscles from shirking work.
Tight Sleeves — Strong human.

Boxing & lumberjack connection: Part 2

In the first volume of the *Boxing Like the Champs* series we discussed Stanley Ketchel's way to build power, throwing boulders. Makes sense. You take a heavy object, heft it and throw it explosively. I'd say that activity contributed mightily to his giant-killing punching prowess. There is a similar activity that comes from the lumberjack tradition and, again, was borrowed by more than a few fighters — the pulp throw.

If you're looking to get outside the comfy smooth gym and test your real mettle with activities and objects that haven't been designed to make hefting them easier, you're gonna love this. Belly up to the bar for a PT challenge from ye olde days of lumberjack and boxing prowess.

Pulp wood was a designation for bucked lengths not quite up to par for lumber use. For our purposes and those into woodsman and lumber sports competitions, grab yourself four lengths of log four feet in length with an approximate weight of 30-40 pounds per. If you don't have logs available, you can hit the resource that is Home Depot and pick up a couple of 6 x 6 pressure treated timbers. They come in 8-foot lengths so a wee middle cut to each gives you a PT resource that will last. They'll be a bit on the light side, but they will serve the purpose.

Course
● Lay out your four pieces of pulp wood.
● Measure out 20 feet.
● Place two stakes four feet apart.

Method
● Stand behind your line 20 feet from the two stakes and toss the pulp so that it lands between the goal stakes.

- For newbies, if you merely get an end length into the staked area, you're good to go.
- For hosses, you'll want to get at least the middle portion of each pulp through the stake line.

Protocol for partners

You stand at one end and your partner at the other.
- You start and throw the four logs though the stake line.
- Upon completion, your partner heaves them back to a stake line on your side of the course.

You will do this for five rounds, for a total of 40 throws, each partner having contributed 20 tosses.

Protocol for solo

Toss your four logs.

Sprint to the opposite stake line and toss 'em back.

Do this for four rounds and a total of 16 throws.

Catch

Whether playing solo or with a partner, as soon as you finish hit a strict 90-second rest then repeat the tosses.

Newbies do this for four rounds

Intermediate for six.

Hosses for eight rounds.

Goal

- Throw fast and furious AND accurately.
- Always shoot for a sub 90-second performance time, always striving to get faster and faster (75 seconds is around your minimum target time for the stout of heart).

Over 90 seconds and you are sandbaggin' or need to go back to the smooth contoured lines of a CrossFit box.

Penalties

Pulp that does not cross the stake line must be retrieved by the thrower and retossed.

Pulp that misses the stakes either to right or left must be retrieved and retossed.

Many an old school boxer, wrestler and rough and tumbler

came from a logging or at the very least a woodsman background. Many of the early competitors in combat sports used actual logging skills as conditioners. You want a piece of that old school, wicked, real world strong don't you? Besides, what looks cooler, you throwing logs like a badass combination man or squatting down and continuously tossing a squishy soft wall ball over your head like a lonely kid with no playmates?

2. Jack Johnson & gandy dancing

If you chose to read this book of your own free will I'd say you know who Jack Johnson is. If you don't, I'm not talking about the laidback singer of bouncy tunes, I'm talking about one of THE greatest ring men who ever lived. Mr. Johnson

Library of Congress

was fast, powerful, slick, and one damn fine technician. And, in the early days at least, superbly conditioned.

Some of that conditioning likely came from his days spent as a gandy dancer. A wha? A gandy dancer was old school slang for men who worked building railroads in the days before automation made such track laying a bit easier. Gandy dancers would lift and carry railroad ties and rails, heap and grade railbeds and drive spikes with powerful swings of the hammer. I'd say that all sounds like a man-size load of work for any man or woman willing to step up and go.

Many a fighter of old adopted a few gandy dancing methods to build strength and power. We'll skip the hammer work this go around as we covered swinging an ax in such depth elsewhere. Here, let's focus on one aspect of gandy dancing that more than a few early fighters swore by—railroad tie lifting.

Gandy dancer circuit for fighters
Gear
● One crosstie.
● At the time of this writing Home Depot, that excellent resource, stocked them for $16.47 before tax. That's a bargain as far as exercise gear goes.
● You can feel free to substitute one of the logs you have hewn with your lumberjack training. You've been doing that, right?

Lifts
Clean
● Get at one end of the tie.
● Squat and place both hands in a cupping manner beneath the end—fingers pointing inward.
  Surge with your squat to upright while using that momentum to sling the crosstie end to shoulder height where you will reverse your hands to catch it on the palms with fingers pointing out.
● Important: You are moving from squat to standing and not merely bending over and lifting with your back.
  Hitting crosstie cleans for a solid round is a good conditioner.

Jerk
  From the top of the clean position…
  Take a slight bend in the knees, say to a 1/4 squat, and then forcibly surge upward taking the crosstie end to be caught in the palms overhead.
  Again, a continuous round of moving from clean to jerk position will set those shoulders on fire.

Clean & jerk
  Here you combine the two into one continuous whole for a greater compound exercise.
  A round of this is stout work.

Lumberjack squat
  From the clean position, lean into the end of the crosstie and squat down until thighs are just below parallel then rise up.
  Try a round of this and see if that don't make you wanna quit.

Clean (1-5) and jerk (6-8). In this sequence the two exercises are performed together (clean & jerk).

Lumberjack thruster
● Another compound exercise.
● Hit the lumberjack squat, but at the top of the squat use the rising momentum to take the tie into overhead position.
  Continuous work with this exercise is a terrific wind builder.

Hand walk, end-over-end
● Take the tie to clean position and then walk the hands towards the center until you allow it to fall over.
● Old-timers would set a distance and then see how quickly they could do this end-over-end walk. One hundred yards is a respectable goal to start.

Waist carry
  This is akin to an awkward deadlift with the instability of movement added.
  Squat at the center of the tie.
  Overhook and underhook the tie and lift it to waist level.
● Now walk while under load.
  Again, distance is a good measure of the exercise. Try 100 yards to start.

Shoulder carry
  A close relation to the previous exercise.
● Clean the tie and hand walk it until you are at the center.
  Settle the tie onto your shoulders and walk under load for distance. Again, 100 yards is a good start.
  Uphill is even better!

Shoulder squat
  Once you have it shouldered and balanced, drop and hit this awkwardly loaded weight for squat reps.

To add gandy dancing training to your boxing conditioning regimen you may combine any of the above into any circuit that you desire or select one exercise per day and wear it out! While you're doing it, you can rest happy in the fact that this worked for some of the best of the best and you are dancing in some of the same gandy footsteps.

Lumberjack squat.

Lumberjack thruster.

Hand walk, end-over-end.

Waist and shoulder carries.

Shoulder squat.

3. Mr. Owen's exertions

Tom "The Fighting Oilman" Owen was a bareknuckle pugilistic champion from the early era. He picked up his title after 50 grueling rounds on November 14, 1796 by defeating William "Bully" Hooper. He has been widely credited with being the inventor of the dumbbell. The credit might be a bit of a stretch as dumbbell-type devices and humans picking up and hefting heavy objects has been going on since man could impress one another with such pursuits.

What is certain is that Owen did indeed utilize the dumbbell in his own training. We have one image of him wearing a top hat and clutching a rather small dumbbell in his right hand. It is surmised that Mr. Owen may have confined his dumbbell work to high reps and a bit of "wind-milling" to build up "bottom" for his fights.

The Fighting Oilman stood five-eight and fought at around 168 pounds. From this stature and what we can surmise from his regimen I offer the following circuit that uses a relatively low weight, but the big movements render the small weight less than small asap.

Protocol (photos 176-177)
● Grasp two dumbbells (you'll know how heavy once you read the circuit description).
● Drop and hit one push-up on the handles.
● Then, supporting yourself on the left dumbbell, lift and extend the right dumbbell skyward while twisting the torso to accommodate. This is a windmill.
● Return it to the ground. That is the first repetition.
● Hit another push-up and repeat the windmill on the other side. That is repetition #2.
● Hit five reps total.

Then...
● Jump to your feet and press (not push-press) the dumbbells overhead.
● Drop and hit the burpee again and repeat the press at the top.
● Hit a total of five burpees to dumbbell presses.

Hit this combination circuit 10 times for a total of 50 push-ups and windmills and 50 burpees to dumbbell presses. Strive to keep movement quality high and the pace up. You get extra credit if your hands never leave the dumbbells. On days where you can't muster the wherewithal for roadwork, you may find this alternative equally horrendous.

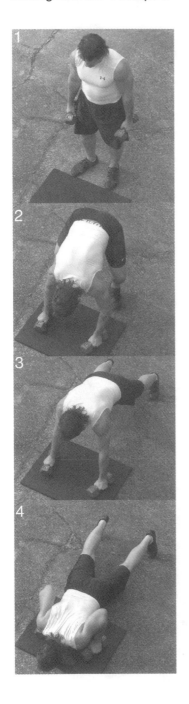

4. Jaw training with
Alan Minter and others

Newsflash: Boxers get punched in the jaw!!!!!!!

The jaw, hinges and chin especially, is a target since it is a fulcrum point for many a knockout. Well placed punches to the jaw can often render an otherwise tremendously conditioned athlete unconscious. Boxers of olde and more than a few today felt that a bit of jaw conditioning allowed them to better able sustain blows to this vital target. The science as to the efficacy of this practice is not definitive, but why not indulge in a little insurance training that takes little time out of your conditioning schedule.

Boxers used to chew pitch in the belief that constantly working the jaw muscles was a good conditioner. Some used a plug of tobacco that they kept moving from side to side for the same reason. Later, fighters adopted chewing large wads of gum with the same end in mind. Chewing gum is a bit of a low-impact activity for such a high impact area. Let's have a look at what some did to up the resistance ante. We'll use the British middleweight of note from the late 1970s Alan Minter as our vanguard.

We'll not delve too much into Mr. Minter's career, but suffice to say he garnered a Bronze Medal as a light middleweight in the 1972 Olympics, and saw a career apex with an undisputed middleweight title in 1980 after having spent some time on the British and European middleweight thrones.

To train his jaw, Minter would take a neck-training, headstrap apparatus and bite into the head strap portion. The weight was never heavy (photos show what appear to be a couple of five pound plates dangling from the chain end). Let's use Minter's idea as a jumping off point.

Jaw warm-up/flexibility

The jaw, like all other portions of a fighter's anatomy, could do with its own warm-up/mobility regimen.

● Open your mouth as wide as possible, hold for a moment, then close the mouth clenching the jaws hard. Hold.
● Repeat five times.
● Shift the jaw from side to side five times.
● Describe small circles with your jaw, five times clockwise, five times counterclockwise.

Jaw clinching.

Jaw side-to-side shifting

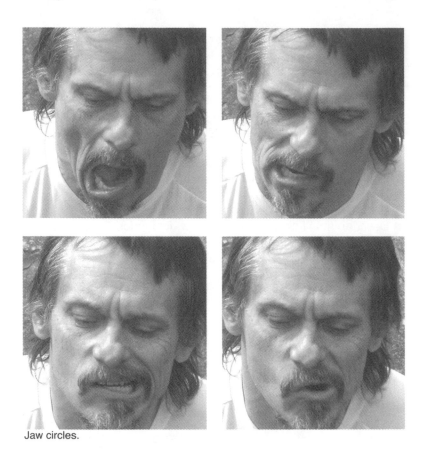

Jaw circles.

Jaw resistance exercises, vertical.

Jaw isometrics

We can garner some strength without apparatus by implementing the following.

● Place your palm beneath your chin and while applying resisting pressure, open your jaw and close it, fighting the pressure on both the positive and negative aspect of the exercise.
● Repeat five times.
● You find that you can also protrude your jaw a bit forward as if in imitation of a bulldog's jaw. Place your palm against the front of your chin and repeat the same resisting pressure regimen fore and aft.
● Repeat five times.
● Place your right palm to the right side of your jaw and use the resisting pressure protocol for a side-to-side movement of the jaw.
● Repeat five times on the right and five on the left.
● Open your mouth wide and place the fingers of one hand over the teeth of the lower jaw. Using slight resisting pressure, fight closing and opening your mouth. Five times.

Use reasonable pressure on all of these, let's not pull any teeth out or dislocate jaws.

Jaw resistance exercises, side to side.

Weight strap work

Now, cribbing from Mr. Minter, grab that weight strap which can be the neck strap itself, or a clean rag attached to your weight strap. Bite that rag and, again, use a reasonable weight, recall Minter only used around 10 pounds.

● *Clench & hold*

Bite the rag and simply hold for time. One minute is a good start. Rather than going up in weight, extending time is the goal here. Work from one minute to a full 3-minute round.

● *Pendulum*

This time bite the rag and slowly swing your head from side to side allowing the inertia of the pendulum swing to add more resistance to the weight bit. Work this swing back and forth for just above comfortable reps. I find that this a good way to finish the timed hold of the preceding exercise.

● *Head rock*

Bite the rag bit and go from looking at the floor to looking overhead. Go slowly on this up and down rock, otherwise you will foul yourself with a ten-pound low blow. Again, a nice way to finish the timed clench.

The efficacy of this is up in the air, but very little time and very little effort for an inch or two of "When you may need it, you got it." Why the hell not?

5. Several roads to neck training

Jaw training's efficacy may be debatable for the fighter, but neck training is a done deal. The head does not sit directly on top of the shoulders, it is stacked on seven cervical vertebrae and the stability (or instability) of this column is dependent on the musculature that holds up that valuable target.

In everyday life most folks have little need of a strong neck, but boxers, wrestlers, and combat sportsmen of all stripes can expect to take some whiplash punishment to the head and it is often the ability of the neck musculature itself to act as dependable shock absorber or stabilizer that spells the difference between weathering something just fine or taking a nap. In the first volume of our foray into old school tips and tactics from the champs we delved into Sonny Liston's method of preparing the neck. Here we will push it further with ideas from the greats that go from the practical to the extreme.

Tried and true: static rear neck bridge.

Static front neck bridge.

Rocking rear neck bridge.

Bridging

Boxers and wrestlers have used bridging for centuries to build the neck, so let's start with this proven standby.

Static rear neck bridge

● Lie on your back and bring the soles of your feet close to your butt.
● Pushing from your feet, rock onto the top of your head. Wrestlers often push this further until the hairline makes mat contact.
● Hold for one minute.

Static front neck bridge

● Flip over and place the top of your head onto the mat and rise up onto the balls of your feet.
● You are simply in the reverse of the prior position.
● Hold for one minute.

Rocking rear neck bridge

● Repeat the steps to get into the static rear neck bridge, but once in bridge position…
● Slowly rock fore and aft.
● Shoot for three sets of 8-10 slooooow repetitions with a full range of motion.

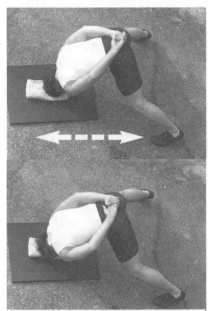

Rocking front neck bridge.

Rocking front neck bridge
● Hit your static front bridge and perform the slow fore-and-aft rocking motions.
● Shoot for three sets of 8-10 slow repetitions, full-range of motion.

Rear side-to-side rock
● From the rear static bridge slowly rock side to side as if you were going to touch each ear alternately to the mat.
● Aim for three sets of 8-10 slow repetitions.
● You need not go for actual ear touches here as the cervical pressure can be a bit extreme, but a small movement can definitely help.

Front side-to-side rock
● I'm betting you know what to do by this point.

The front and rear neck bridge in both the rocking and static permutations primarily condition the trapezius, or rear neck musculature and does little for the sternocleidomastoid muscles that tether your neck from approximate jaw hinge to the clavicle region. To remedy this oversight, try the following *(next page)*.

Rear side-to-side rocking neck bridge.

185

Front wall rock
● Place your forehead against either a padded wall or place a pillow against the wall and press your forehead into it.
● Using steady pressure from your feet, slowly nod your head fore and aft.
● Use the same repetition, set and full range-of-motion protocol as in the mat versions of the exercise.

Weighted bridging & rocking

All of the preceding exercises can be increased in difficulty by clutching a dumbbell or weight plate to the chest while performing the exercise. Most will find very slow rocking sets followed by a one-minute static hold enough to do the job, but if you have progressed to a point where more seems better, feel free to add weight.

Side-to-side press.

Side-to-side press

So far we have only worked the neck in a fore and aft and ear-to-ear manner, but that still leaves "looking left and right" conditioning untouched.

All hooks to the jaw will forcibly torque the head along the look-left/look-right plane so we need to address that as well.
● Turn your head all the way left and place your right palm against the right side of your jaw.
● Slowly turn your head to the right while fighting with hand pressure.
● Be sure to apply pressure on both the positive and negative aspects of the motion.
● Hit 8-10 slow repetitions of this, then do the same on the opposite side.
● Do three sets of this sequence.

Weight straps

Many boxers have used a weighted neck strap to condition the neck, but they only work along the fore-and-aft plane for the back of the neck and do nothing for the side-to-side (ear-to-ear) range, nothing for the sternocleidomastoids, nor the "look-left/look-right" plane. It is for this very limitation that I view the neck strap as a limited option for neck training. I think you'll find the bridging options outlined above more than enough to build a strong and stable shock-absorbing, stabilizing neck musculature.

A few more neck options: extreme flavor

The preceding chapter on neck training is one I have no problem offering to most all combat athletes, but I can't be as blithe about the following options. Each was used by a few champs in the past so who am I to argue with them, but, well, you'll see, it's up to you and your own discretion if any of these ideas strike you as sound. Let's take them in order as they ascend the scale from tough to absolutely nuts.

Ignacio Pina's corner headstand

Mexican bantamweight southpaw, Ignacio Zurda Pina, used a variation of Sonny Liston's headstand method for neck training. He would...

● Place a towel on the canvas in a ring corner.
● Place his head on the towel and pop up into a standard headstand.
● Once there he would hook his calves over the top rope and then go to a hands-free headstand and perform minor rocking to build his neck.

If one has a mind to try this, might I recommend at least three months of neck training using the methods in the prior chapter before advancing to this stage.

Larry Gains & the neck step

Larry "The Toronto Terror" Gains, a very active heavyweight from 1923 until 1942, used to...

● Lie on the canvas on first his right side and...
● Have his trainer step onto the side of his neck while he clenched his neck muscles fighting the weight.
● He would then roll to the other side and repeat said practice. I have no info on how heavy his trainer was, but if you are going to give this a go, might I suggest treading lightly.

Jack Dempsey & the hangman

OK, this one is a little out there. Make that way out there.

I can't run down evidence that Dempsey tried this himself, but there is a photo of him with trainer Ernie Dusek with Mr. Dempsey holding one end of a rope that goes up and over a rafter while at the other end Mr. Dusek, wearing his wrestling trunks and boots, is happily suspended by his neck. Ernie Dusek was a professional wrestler who also conditioned a few boxers here and there. Dusek wrestled during the hazy transition from real wrestling to sports entertainment. He undoubtedly participated in entertainment bouts, but he also had real-deal skills.

Wrestlers have long valued neck training and Dusek was not the only proponent of hangman's noose training. Noted wrestling patriarch Martin "Farmer" Burns also used to "hang" himself regularly as part of his demonstrations.

May I make the following suggestion? Don't do this. Notice there is no photo of me demonstrating this. Nor will there ever be. Reader, let's you and I form a pact and agree that this is one lesson from the champs we are happy to know from afar.

6. "The Herkimer Hurricane" push & shove drill

Lou Ambers, a two-time lightweight champion, was born in 1913 in Herkimer, New York, hence one half of his ring name. Lou was one of those fighters who skipped amateur bouts and jumped right into being a pro. Usually without early experience one would suffer with this jump directly to the big leagues, but Mr. Ambers racked up 32 straight victories at the beginning of his career. This pro jump and success rate did not go unnoticed as he was ranked the 9th best lightweight contender in 1933, a mere year after getting into the game.

Lest we think that he stepped fully formed out of the womb, what Ambers did in place of amateur bouts was potentially a more formidable school of hard knocks. He fought many a "bootleg" fight before his pro debut. This is essentially off-the-books bouts where anyone with heart could be grist for the fight-viewing entertainment mill. Mr. Ambers, in the phraseology of the old days, "had been through the mill and he don't grind fine." In other words, he paid his dues and gave better than he got.

The second half of that awkward ring name referred to his work rate. He worked fast and furious. But he was no mere slugger despite what that bootleg school might imply. He was a vastly clever boxer. There are many lessons we could take from Mr. Ambers, but the one we shall focus on for this volume is an interestingly non-violent method of drilling that he used to work power, footwork, balance, wind, and punch positioning.

For this one, all you need is yourself and a partner. No gloves or even mouthpiece required.

Protocol: Phase One *(photos 192-193)*
● Face each other in stance.
● Take turns placing either a lead or rear palm on the other's upper body and push hard.
● Don't use a mere shoving motion, think punch extension mechanics.
● Work this alternately while moving about the training area.

This shoving allows you to find how to set your feet upon punch impact and, on the flipside, allows you to find balance while you are being shoved. This drill is a win-win in that regard.

Phase Two
● This time face your partner in a left lead stance, you both fire lead palms to the chest simultaneously, then...
● Once contact has been made, quickly switch stance to right lead forward and fire the new lead palm to the chest.
● Do this back and forth at a furious space and tell me it doesn't light up the heart and lungs.
● Learn to see your way to landing in the slow-motion tussle (slow motion compared to actual sparring).

It is an ideal drill to warm up with, to cool down with, to use when the bags are full or to break the monotony of banging the pads. I might add this is a great intro for gunshy rookies to get used to the scrum without the concomitant impact. Again, this deceptively simple drill allows both fighters to find balance, find how to set their feet for power, how to brace the body for impact, and it can bump the sweat rate if both are willing to keep a Herkimer Hurricane pace.

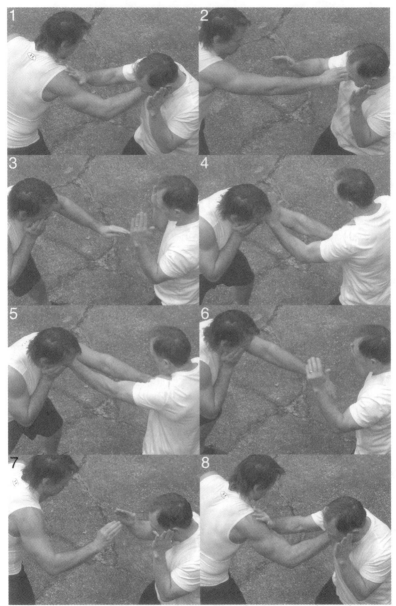

Pushing & shoving—Taking turns placing either a lead or rear palm on the other's upper body and pushing hard.

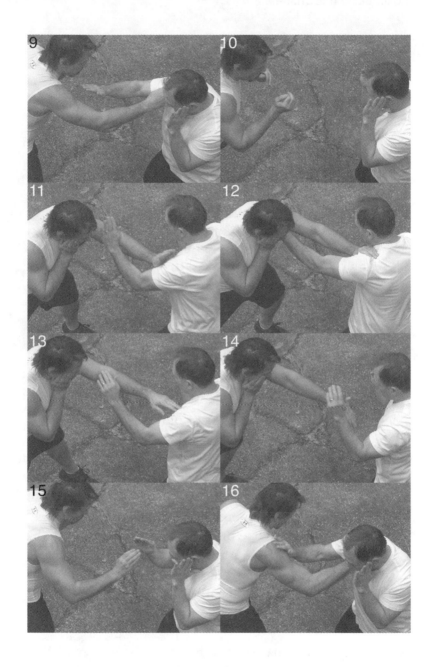

7. A dip in the pool with Giovanni "Nino" Benvenuti & others

We're going to allow the Italian middleweight champion with matinee idol good looks to be our lifeguard in this exploration of boxers using water or pool work to augment their training. Mr. Benvenuti was born in Trieste, Italy in 1938. His was an athletic family, four boys all of whom aspired to the ring. This family affair served Nino well as he had 120 amateur bouts in Italy and lost zero. He held the middleweight championship on three different occasions and his three fights with fellow Boxing Hall-of-Famer Emile Griffith are mighty instructive.

What we will take from Mr. Benvenuti this time is not inside-the-ropes tactical so much as outside-the-ropes conditioning.

Nino was a good all-around athlete and he made swimming a large part of his conditioning regimen. Swimming, at the time, was not commonly used so it was noteworthy to many contemporary boxing journalists. It still isn't quite as commonly practiced as the more traditional roadwork, but we are seeing more and more top-notch athletes embrace it. We see fighters from the Klitschko brothers to Floyd Mayweather Jr. doing pool work as well as Amir Khan, Manny Pacquiao and Miguel Cotto. There is a growing cadre of fighters who use water work equally with roadwork and a few, like Juan Diaz, who never run and just swim.

Many aging fighters have stated that they wished they had come to it earlier as roadwork is mighty hard on the knees over time (I can attest to that). The no-impact nature of the activity is manna for those seeking an injury-free exercise. And lest anyone think that water work is less grueling than roadwork, well, according to the pros, you simply ain't doing it right. It can eat you alive.

Water work options for fighters

Water-boxing warm-up

This is an easy option to begin and end a water session with, or an alternative for the non-swimmers out there.

Immerse into chest deep water and shadowbox fast and furiously for your designated rounds of choice.

The water's resistance adds a bit of fun to the game.

Water-boxing immersion sprint

The same concept as the preceding, but here you take a deep breath and submerge into water over your head and throw furiously for 15 seconds.

Rest for 30 seconds.

Repeat for a total of eight 15-second rounds.

By this point we begin to have an appreciation for the subtleties and utility of water work.

Viking sprints

Another excellent lung and leg burner and ideal for our non-swimming compatriots.

Find a stretch of shoreline that is around mid-thigh depth.

● Pick out a stretch of 100-yard straightaway and run it as fast as possible.

● You'll find you'll have to pick those knees up high to get any simulacra of speed and, if you are in a natural body of water, the pliable nature of the soil, sand and mud beneath your feet adds even more resistance.

Shoot for five Viking sprints with a minute rest in between.

Swim sprints

Grab a lane in the pool or in open water and shoot for an approximate 50 meters.

● Swim sprint as quickly as possible.

● Don't worry if your technique is poor. You will still suck wind whether you've got triathlete technique or not. Just get in and do the work.
● Shoot for 10 sprints total with one minute of rest between.

Medium haul
● Grab a lane or, better yet, open water for this one.
● Pick a nice medium distance for your skill level, 1/4 mile is a nice start, and get out there and go.
● Find your pace, don't drown, and utilize the universal wisdom of a swim buddy or friend in a canoe alongside you if you get into trouble.

Long haul
You can use a pool, but open water will change your dynamic in useful ways. You will have to account for tide, current and waves and it cannot be overemphasized that there is something a bit elemental about simply getting out there where there is no easy ledge to reach for.

Again, swim buddy or kayaking partner is a must.
● Pick a distance that fits you, 1/2 mile may not sound like much if you've never swam, but you'll see.

Hit the water and keep going.

Submerged sprints
Working sans oxygen is a stressor, so being a fighter you want a piece of that, right?

Hit the pool or open water and pick out a distance around half of what you do above water. So, let's shoot for around 25 meters or 25 yards.

Hold your breath, submerge and knock out that distance lickety-split.

Rest one minute and repeat for a total of eight rounds.

Swimming is an excellent conditioning spice to add to your game. Or as some fighters are increasingly doing, making it a big part of the game. Even if you don't go so far as to allow it to replace roadwork, adding a little water work will put miles in the tank all the same.

Viking sprints.

8. Blitz-drills "The Hawk" style

First, hold this number in your mind: 130. We'll come back to it.

...that's how Mr. Pryor worked. He W-O-R-K-E-D. He didn't simply throw fast and often, he threw HARD.

Aaron "The Hawk" Pryor. Anyone who has a good eye and memory for great boxers of the late '70s and early '80s is likely already salivating at the name of Aaron Pryor. Pryor held both a junior welterweight and a welterweight title at one time.

He left an amateur career that saw 220 fights with 204 wins, picking up two National Golden Gloves titles along the way. His pro career included 24 straight wins, 22 by KO. He was to stay on that streak until derailed by a chaotic lifestyle out of the ring. He retired with a 39 and 1 record.

His style was described at the time as "thrilling," "ceaseless," and at times marked by "reckless abandon." Mr. Pryor showed up to fight. He was an excellent boxer, but make no mistake he was there to throw. He was there to work. And work he did.

Back to that number "130." In 1982 he was to put his title on the line against the very capable challenger Alexis Arguello. The Hawk threw 130 punches in the first round alone. This fight was no anomaly, that's how Mr. Pryor worked. He W-O-R-K-E-D. He didn't simply throw fast and often, he threw HARD. For this lesson, we'll take just one aspect of Mr. Pryor's gorgeous game—his work rate—and apply a few drills to get us up to speed, as it were.

Aaron Pryor blitz drills
Most of us will not be used to this level of energy expenditure, but the following drills are meant to get us there.

The Protocol
You will use 30-second rounds and 90-seconds of rest. Sounds a bit on the light side, doesn't it? But if you are doing it right, giving all you got in each of these mini-round blitzes, you'll know what's what after round one.

Round 1
● Throw nonstop, rapid-fire jabs and rear straights as hard and fast as the heart will allow.

Round 2
● Repeat with lead and rear hooks to head level.

Round 3
● Repeat with lead and rear hooks to the body.

Round 4
● Repeat with lead and rear uppercuts to the body.

That is a mere two minutes of "on time" work. If you've done it right, you should be sucking wind like nobody's business. We have not sought to deepen the combination number or to increase complexity simply because we do not want anything to get in the way of GO!

Pryor was able to blitz and have great technique at the same time. We want to strive for that ideal as well. But we'll allow our other boxing lessons to be a more sedate appreciation of the perfections and use these blitz drills to grab a bit of the Hawk's mind-staggering velocity.

Jab/ cross.

Lead and rear hooks.

Lead and rear uppercuts. Throw each combo fast and hard!

Final round?

I gotta say, I hate to see this book end. I love deep Mariana Trench dives into the past masters and these two books have been absolute pleasures to work on. Have we exhausted the material from the past? Oh, hell no!

But we got to hang the "Closed" sign up some time and get some sleep. When we open our doors again perhaps we will examine a few things we didn't get to in this second round of historical fun.

For example, we didn't...
- Get inside with "The Fargo Express."
- Break down the short wallop of a rear hook that belonged to "The Black Uhlan."
- Reconstruct Ike William's canny defense.
- Get inside the timing and fearsome power of Carlos Zarate.
- Catalog the astounding "off the books" tactics of Fritzie Zivic.
- See through the eyes of Eddie Futch.
- Get into "Solid Man" condition, William Muldoon style.
- Talk about the connection between temperature and fight training with Charley Goldman and Emanuel Steward.
- Develop the "retreating mill" of Tom Cribb.
- Learn to throw Nat Langham's "pickaxe."
- Build power with Charlie Burley.
- Break down a fighter like Al Silvani

Well, we could go on and on. A round three in this series is not out of the question as there is so much to be mined in the past. One more time, the quote from the introduction that we opened this volume with:

"Those who cannot remember the past are condemned to repeat it."

After having read these pages and the others in this series, I sincerely hope you have condemned yourself to a future that repeats these gorgeous lessons of the past!

For more information, books, DVDs, training resources and opportunities with the author visit our website at:
http://www.extremeselfprotection.com

Where I did my digging

I have read old boxing texts, articles, memoirs and chased down old fight footage for years upon years and to be honest I can't recall every single hole where I dug up a gorgeous nugget of gold. But the list of texts on the next page has provided many a rich vein.

And perhaps most importantly, there were treasures found in antique shops, old attics and grandfathers' sea chests that included tattered and coverless copies of *Boxing & Wrestling Magazine, Boxing Illustrated & Wrestling News, Fight Stories, The Ring, Jack Dempsey's Fight Magazine* and many others.

I'll keep digging and keep on offering what the fertile ground offers.

Till the next time!

A Selected Bibliography

Fleischer, Nat and Andre, Sam. A Pictorial History of Boxing. Secaucus, New Jersey: Citadel Press, 1987.

Fried, Ronald K. Corner Men: Great Boxing Trainers. New York, New York: DeCapo Press, 1993.

Gems, Gerald R. Boxing: A Concise History of the Sweet Science. Lanham, Maryland: Rowman & Littlefield Publishers, 2014.

Golding, Louis. The Bare Knuckle Breed. London: Hutchinson Publishing, 1952.

Gorn, Elliott J. The Manly Art: Bare-Knuckle Prize Fighting in America. Ithaca, New York: Cornell University Press, 2010.

Heller, Peter. "In This Corner..." 42 World Champions Tell Their Stories. New York, New York: DeCapo Press, 1994.

Lardner, Rex. The Legendary Champions. Winter Park, Florida: American Heritage Press, 1972.

Mee, Bob. Bare Fists. New York, New York: Harpercollins Publishers, 2000.

O'Brien, Richard. The Boxing Companion: An Illustrated Guide to the Sweet Science. New York, New York: Bdd Promotional Book Company, 1991.

Roberts, James B. and Skutt, Alexander G. The Boxing Register. Ithaca, New York: McBooks Press, 2011.

Index

Mark Hatmaker is the bestselling author of the *No Holds Barred Fighting Series*, the *MMA Mastery Series*, *No Second Chance* and *Boxing Mastery*. He also has produced more than 40 instructional videos. His resume includes extensive experience in the combat arts including boxing, wrestling, Jiu-jitsu and Muay Thai.

He is a highly regarded coach of professional and amateur fighters, law enforcement officials and security personnel. Hatmaker founded Extreme Self Protection (ESP), a research body that compiles, analyzes and teaches the most effective Western combat methods known. ESP holds numerous seminars throughout the country each year including the prestigious Karate College/Martial Arts Universities in Radford, Virginia. He lives in Knoxville, Tennessee.

www.extremeselfprotection.com

Tracks Publishing
Ventura, California